5 Marks of Christian Resolve
by C. Matthew McMahon

Copyright Information

5 Marks of Christian Resolve by C. Matthew McMahon
Edited by Therese B. McMahon

Copyright ©2020 by Puritan Publications and A Puritan's Mind®

Some language and grammar are updated from any original manuscripts. Any change in wording or punctuation has not changed the intent or meaning of the original author(s) and has been made to aid the modern reader.

Published by Puritan Publications
A Ministry of A Puritan's Mind® in Crossville, TN.
www.apuritansmind.com
www.puritanpublications.com

All rights reserved. No part of this publication may be reproduced, stored in a retrieval system or transmitted in any form by any means, electronic, mechanical, photocopy, recording or otherwise, without the prior permission of the publisher, except as provided by USA copyright law.

This Print Edition, 2020
Electronic Edition, 2020

Manufactured in the United States of America

ISBN: 978-1-62663-387-2
eISBN: 978-1-62663-386-5

Table of Contents

Introduction 4

MARK 1: Resolved to Work to the Glory of God 10

MARK 2: Resolved to Contend for the Faith 37

MARK 3: Resolved to Reject Earthlimindedness 60

MARK 4: Resolved in the Means of Grace 81

MARK 5: Resolved to Continue to Do Good 107

Other Books in the 5 Marks Series 136

Introduction:
What is it to be Resolved?

"I am resolved what to do..." (Luke 16:4).

Being *resolved* is a biblical precedent to all our holy actions. It is, actually, a *non-negotiable* precedent if godly actions will in fact take place after making the resolution. Interestingly, we begin our study on "resolution" by applying the idea of that word "resolved" to five tenants that Christians ought to be resolved in. However, our initial Scripture (Luke 16:4) came forth in the parable that Christ gave about the *unjust* steward who was resolved, after much deliberation, to cast himself on the mercy of the Master. This is good spiritual practice from such an unworthy fellow. But Christ says that the children of the world are more shrewd than the sons of light, as he ends this parable. The children of light do not, as they should, resolve to follow the Master as the unjust steward did. That means, you and I, reader, as children of light, don't' act as shrewdly as the unjust steward did. That's a sad commentary on us. On a basic level, Christ's teaching was to direct his hearers to throw themselves completely and without reservation on his mercy. This takes shrewdness, and this unjust steward resolved, deliberated, *made resolution* after considering everything he needed to, to *set down a plan* that would in fact be successful. And in all this, *making* the resolution was not enough. He needed to put into action what he resolved to do. This begs the statement of Christ, "The spirit is willing but the flesh is weak," as it concerns children of light.

Resolutions are *not* the actions of resolve themselves; they are only the beginning of what one resolves to do. Many people make New Year's *resolutions*, and most of them fizzle out before they ever get started. If you think about it, there is nothing that we do which is commendable if we *merely resolve* to do something. If we resolve to do something, and never actually get around to doing it, what good is that? Being resolved, in and of itself, is as a false conception that is buried in the birth of a holy idea, and does not come to execution except by the power of the Spirit of God motioning the soul to be "up and doing". Again, hear the words of Christ, "...the spirit indeed is willing, but the flesh is weak," (Matt. 26:41). Willing is one thing, but *doing* is something more. If the farmer is always fixing his equipment, always spending time in preparing to *do* something, and never actually gets around to *tilling* the ground, will he ever be able to sow or reap anything of value? A weak and wobbling resolution in this way, holds in it nothing of real value. And if such a resolve is made, but it is weak in its parts, the outcome will be that as soon as the work is *well intended*, then our resolution ends, and our work should begin. In such a work we desire to glorify the living Christ in *service*. But service does, truly, come *after* resolution, yet in light of it.

Introduction: What is it to be Resolved?

In considering this, there is oftentimes more difficulty in *making* a resolution, than in *following through and doing* what one resolves to do. For a true and Spirit-guided resolution to take place, the Christian mind considers *many things*. It deliberates many things all at once to consider everything that ought to be considered in accomplishing the work. But, when that resolution gives birth to a Spirit-empowered work, that then places the resolved conscience into action, and the action itself has begun the work. It is focused in diversities and contrarieties in resolving to do something, but fortified in the action once the action takes place. That Christian is then set to do what he has resolved to do.

Many times, Christians are tortured in their mind in resolving to do something, where, then, as they *engage* in a resolute work, they then find peace; beginning the actual work eases their desire to resolve to do something, and breeds confidence. There the unjust steward planned and contrived a work, and then when *resolved* to do it, he found peace in its outcome being confident that his plan was sound. It takes a lot of planning to *make good* a good work. A solid, biblical, Spirit-filled resolution gives the Christian no rest until they put their hand on the plough to till, or to do the work itself, in whatever way it should fall out, into practice. Yet, be assured, that all true resolution turns all *resolving powers into execution.*

Having a resolve to do something is a wonderful beginning. It ties two parts of a duty together for the Christian; to resolve *and* do. To do something without resolution to the action is rashness. To resolve without doing the work is slightness. The one who does a work without resolution thinks there will be no impediments to their work (deceiving himself). One who resolves and delays doing the work waits *on* impediments, and this too is a hindrance; they never get around to doing anything in the Kingdom of God.

What, then, is it to *be resolved?* Resolution is a fixed determination of the will about anything, either to do it, or not to do it, with a due deliberation to judge and conclude the action to be necessary, or convenient to be done, or not to be done by us as befitting the glory of God. That is a mouthful, but it is *important.* It may even be that such a definition be read over again a few times to let it sink in (take some time to do that).

Being resolved as a Christian, sets forth a deliberation of the mind about the thing to be resolved on. No wise Christian will ever resolve to do anything until he has considered the action, and weighed it in the balance of Scripture within himself, and fully debated its necessity and expedience. It will bring in the clarity of judgment he passes on the thing to be done, after he has deliberated about it. He will be satisfied in his mind one way or the other concerning it, convinced that it is necessary and convenient for him to do it, or that it is not. In this, there is knowledge acting both on prudence,

Introduction: What is it to be Resolved?

and emotion. If the action to be accomplished is of considerable consequence (such as doing good to fellow believers), there is some motion of the affections which is a kind of bias on the will, a certain inclination that a person feels in himself, either urging him to do it, or withdrawing him from it. And what Christian would, then, be drawn *away* from doing good to the household of faith? Only those who have not rightly considered or deliberated the work itself; those without biblical resolution. Especially as it regards the things of Christ's kingdom, people ought to be well aware of what they are doing, and why they are doing it. In this, there is a great resolve set down (a determination of the will), and action (a manifestation of the will's deliberation) that follows the resolve in order to be "up and doing" for the glory of Christ. Such resolve in general is a fixed determination of the will, which then gives birth to holy action.

When a Christian resolves in this way to please God in some virtuous and holy service, they meet with many difficulties, and are often required to deny themselves, which, for holy service to God, they would gladly comply with. However, if they are fully bent on Christ's ways, and knit to him by a fixed resolution and steady purpose of obedience, and then they waiver, the good that they are seeking in any holy action, may be lost by doubt and uncertainty.

How might a Christian be resolved in the work of doing good *always* before God so as to throw off doubt and uncertainty in the resolution? And in what main categories might resolution take place? In considering a holy resolve, a fixed determination of serving King Jesus, this book will cover five marks: Mark 1: resolved to do great works for the glory of God in everything. Mark 2: resolved to contend for the faith once delivered to the saints. Mark 3: resolved to reject all earthlimindedness. Mark 4: resolved to righteously use the means of grace for further sanctification as Christ prescribes. Mark 5: resolved to continue to do good without growing weary.

It is certainly true that every Christian duty may be placed under the auspice of being "resolved" to do it to the glory of God. Such important aspects as repentance, exercising faith, godly prayer and bible devotions, godly meditation, church attendance, hearing the word preached, *etc.*, all should comprise a fixed deliberation *to be done*, and *done well* to God's glory. But a volume of this size cannot encompass every point, and must, of necessity, speak comparatively brief for the success of the overall point. Suffice if for now, to apply the idea of *resolve* biblically in the five marks outlined above, and that a sincere resolution is set down on a firm assent to the truth of Christ's revelation in Scripture. From this point, all subsequent ideas derive their help in the following pages.

MARK 1: Resolved to Do Great Works for the Glory of God

Nehemiah 6:1-4, "Now it came to pass, when Sanballat, and Tobiah, and Geshem the Arabian, and the rest of our enemies, heard that I had builded the wall, and that there was no breach left therein; (though at that time I had not set up the doors upon the gates;) That Sanballat and Geshem sent unto me, saying, Come, let us meet together in some one of the villages in the plain of Ono. But they thought to do me mischief. And I sent messengers unto them, saying, I am doing a great work, so that I cannot come down: why should the work cease, whilst I leave it, and come down to you? Yet they sent unto me four times after this sort; and I answered them after the same manner."

This narrative concerning Ezra and Nehemiah took place around 431 A.D., where Nehemiah begins in exile. What does it mean to be a Babylonian exile? Exile was generally a result of apostasy from God and his worship, and breaking his covenant. Israel and Judah are seen throughout Old Testament history as *continually* displeasing God, and God bringing judgment on them, though he loved them as his people and church (Jeremiah 3:1). If a people do not walk with God, if his worship is not upheld, if he is forced out of his sanctuary

(Ezek. 8:6), God *judges* his people.[1] Yet, such judgment always rests in the promise to bring them back to himself and fix all the breaches of their sin through his anointed Messiah. Psalm 137:8, "O daughter of Babylon, who are to be destroyed, Happy the one who repays you as you have served us! Happy the one who takes and dashes your little ones against the rock!" Dashing children against the rocks is a figurative phrase, but it demonstrates the heinous nature of how exile *is terrible*. The Psalmist desires to dash the babies of the foreign nations against the rocks. That is as disgusting as exile is appalling. One is stripped of their home, families, possessions, and many times their lives. They become slaves, are taken against their will, and deprived of their very culture, pressed to conform to the ways of the heathen nations.[2]

Nehemiah's countenance after a time of exile was low. There was breaking news which had come to him. "And they said to me, "The survivors who are left from the captivity in the province are there in great distress and reproach. The wall of Jerusalem is also broken down, and its gates are burned with fire." So it was, when I heard these words, that I sat down and wept, and mourned for many days; I was fasting and praying before the God of heaven," (Neh. 1:3-4). Nehemiah had great

---

[1] Consider Leviticus 26 in light of the coronavirus all over the world today.
[2] "Thus saith the LORD, Learn not the way of the heathen, and be not dismayed at the signs of heaven; for the heathen are dismayed at them," (Jer. 10:2).

sadness before the King of Babylon (2:1). He was a cup bearer for the king. At this time, though, his sadness was so apparent, that the king took notice. "Now I had never been sad in his presence before. Therefore the king said to me, "Why is your face sad, since you are not sick? This is nothing but sorrow of heart,"" (Neh. 2:1-2). It was difficult for a worshipping people to be in a foreign land – to be away from the temple, the place of God's "nearness". God's presence was lost, and God's displeasure was now felt. There was no worship, no sacrifice, no comfort now. Nehemiah knew, though, God was a listening God, (Neh. 1:5-6), "I pray…" He knew that God would keep covenant. He knew that God would have mercy. He knew God would be attentive. "Let your ear be attentive…" There, in his prayer closet, he could have hope.

Nehemiah's desire was to rebuild the wall of Jerusalem and occupy the city again. Why such a fascination about a wall? Building *the wall* of Jerusalem? It was in fact a secret desire he had (2:11-12). It was important because God had placed this desire in Nehemiah's heart. This was an eye to the worship of God restored – and in this Nehemiah desired comfort. True comfort only reveals itself in true worship, in being drawn close to God and God drawing close to him. Nehemiah's very name *means*, "Yahweh is Comfort." He was looking to be comforted by God, for himself, and his people.

Nehemiah looked to build a boundary that surrounds the worship of God in the center of religion, in the center of Jerusalem. It was like the hug of God around the temple, so to speak. If God would just allow them to go back and fix *that wall*, he would again show his favor to his wayward people. He would be calling them home.

Nehemiah is allowed by the king to go, and take a necessary convoy with him; an amazing providence. He leaves and journeys to Jerusalem to rebuild the wall. He goes to restore worship. He will use Ezra the Scribe to bring the people back to the word of God, and to preach, and to teach, and to restore true and undefiled worship. This would be to bring the people back to walking with God. This was the *great work* he would put his hand to. The work of the wall was in direct connection with the establishment of true religious worship that God prescribed. Nehemiah was "really" engaging in bringing back the *Regulative Principle of Worship* for the people by securing the city.[3]

---

[3] "John Calvin says, "God has been pleased to prescribe in his law what is lawful and right, and thus astrict men to a certain rule, lest any should allow themselves to devise a worship of their own." This is a good representation of what the *Regulative Principle* teaches. The Regulative Principle was given its classical and definitive statement throughout the Reformed Confessions formulated in the 17th century. It is stated in chapter 21 paragraph 1 in the *1647 Westminster Confession*, "The light of nature showeth that there is a God, who hath lordship and sovereignty over all, is good, and doth good unto all, and is therefore to be feared, loved, praised, called upon, trusted in, and served, with all the heart, and with all the soul, and with all the might.[1] But the acceptable way of worshiping the true God is instituted by himself, and so limited by his own revealed

Mark 1: Resolved to Do Great Works for the Glory of God

What *was* Nehemiah's great work? Was it merely to build the wall? When the wall was to be built, when the enemies of God heard that it was actually occurring, they tried to their utmost to hinder that work and kill Nehemiah. It is true, without a vision, people go astray. The enemies were right – kill Nehemiah and it will hinder the vision of the people, cause them to be despondent that God would allow their governor to die, and the work on the wall *may* cease. When they tried to entrap him, he sent word back to them countering their desire to overthrow the work. "So I sent messengers to them, saying, "I am doing a great work, so that I cannot come down. Why should the work cease while I leave it and go down to you?" But they sent me this message four times, and I answered them in the same manner," (Neh. 6:3-4). These enemies intended to do him harm, and hinder God's work, but a "great" work had begun (6:3), and it could not be stopped. Building a wall is a great work? Is *construction* a great work? This work was a means to an end, and within this work was another work. In Neh. 4:9 in this great work they were to "watch

---

will, that he may not be worshiped according to the imaginations and devices of men, or the suggestions of Satan, under any visible representation, or any other way not prescribed in the Holy Scripture.[2] (1. Rom. 1:20; Psa. 19:1-4a; 50:6; 86:8-10; 89:5-7; 95:1-6; 97:6; 104:1-35; 145:9-12; Acts 14:17; Deut. 6:4-5. 2. Deut. 4:15-20; 12:32; Matt. 4:9-10; 15:9; Acts 17:23-25; Exod. 20:4-6, John 4:23-24; Col. 2:18-23.)" The Westminster Confession follows Reformed Theology as outlined in Calvin's tract. McMahon, C. Matthew, *The Reformed Apprentice: A Workbook on Reformed Theology*, (Coconut Creek, FL: Puritan Publications, 2013) section on *Reforming the Church.*

and pray." It reads, "Nevertheless we made our prayer to our God, and because of them we set a watch against them day and night," (Neh. 4:9). They had a sword in one hand and a trowel in the other. Nehemiah would not give up that which God put in his heart, and the work he was currently engaged in which was a *very* great work (Neh. 6:3).

The words "come down" which he responds to the letter, are used both literally and morally. Come down off the wall, is what they wanted him to do. But it holds the idea that it would have been a *descending to a lower moral level*. Not to be raised up, but pressed down, having a highly negative connotation. The work will cease if Nehemiah *comes down*. Literally "cease" means to utterly stop in every sense of the word. In commitment, resolution, desire, and physical work. It is the same word used that God uses in the command to put to an end to work that on the Lord's Day, in "ceasing" from work, to put down that work and pick up God's work (*cf.* Exodus 20). So, Nehemiah's resolve is to continue the work no matter what. An unresolved heart wanders from place to place, but God's steward resolved to stand firm, and will not allow the work to stop, much less even to slow down.

God's people here remembered that great works done for God must never cease. Nehemiah's eminent piety before God set him to resolve all things to him and do the great work given to him with an eye toward true biblical reformation and the purity of religious worship.

Mark 1: Resolved to Do Great Works for the Glory of God

In such a *resolve* great works have great events occur, even great endings to their purpose and goal in the narrative; and according to 6:16, success was given by God's power (Neh. 6:16). This was not only *known*, but experientially *seen*. "So the wall was finished on the twenty-fifth day of Elul, in fifty-two days. And it happened, when all our enemies heard of it, and all the nations around us saw these things, that they were very disheartened in their own eyes; for they perceived that this work was done by our God," (Neh. 6:15-16).

Nehemiah had continued opposition in this great work. "Now it happened when Sanballat, Tobiah, Geshem the Arab, and the rest of our enemies heard that I had rebuilt the wall, and that there were no breaks left in it (though at that time I had not hung the doors in the gates), that Sanballat and Geshem sent to me, saying, "Come, let us meet together among the villages in the plain of Ono." But they thought to do me harm," (Neh. 6:2). Like Judas Iscariot, they took the disposition of a kiss, and yet, meant to kill him; they were trying to appear as a friend, for peace, but really were enemies to the work of God. Nehemiah, in opposition, draws a line in the sand. When such deceit came knocking on his door, he stood firm. Deception and treachery did not come once, or twice, but four times. They wanted him to journey to the plain of Ono, (6:4, *four times* mentioned). This would have drawn him a good distance away from Jerusalem. The intent was always to get him off the work. The intent was to do him harm. The intent was to *kill him*. The intent was to stop the great work being done for God.

There are three main points to consider in this resolution to do great works for God, and *point 1* is: all duties accomplished for God and Christ by faith *are* a great work for the Christian.

What does it mean that something is a "great" work? Great works are always *great by way of faith*. Whatever is not of faith is sin.[4] Great works are never without faith, and all great works have an effect on eternity.[5] These are *great*, not only in magnitude, but also in importance, since they are connected to eternal realities. This is not because of something the Christian *sees* in the work that is great, but that the work which he does before God *is great* because *God is great who commands it*. The very fact that God tells Christians to do something, makes that "something" a great work. There are two motivations for this. God's greatness as the Great King who command his people before him, as well as the Christian's required imitation of Christ's resolve as the perfect man who fulfilled all things perfectly as God's fellow.

First, God is great in and of himself which is the Christian's chief motivation to all duty. Neh. 1:5, "And said, I beseech thee, O LORD God of heaven, the great and terrible God," Neh. 8:6, "And Ezra blessed the LORD, the great God." Nehemiah knew God was great.

---

[4] Rom. 14:23.
[5] 2 Cor. 4:17; 2 Peter 2:13; Rev. 22:12.

Mark 1: Resolved to Do Great Works for the Glory of God

Could any work *for God* be less than great? God is great in and of himself. "Behold, God is great, and we do not know him; Nor can the number of his years be discovered," (Job 36:26). Some people have said, "God said it, I believe it, that settles it." No, no; that is a quite mistaken phrase used through all of Christendom today. It needs to be corrected. Rather, *God said it, that settles it.* Men are not included in the enlargement of the "greatness of a thing pertaining to God's holiness or righteousness." Whether *men* believe something is a great work or not is not the issue. If God said it, that in and of itself, *completely and utterly settles it.* And because *he* said it, *it is a great work,* whatever that work might be.

The Bible depicts God as the Most High God, Lord of heaven and earth, where everything that exists is under God's kingly rule.[6] And God vocally, and by way of the written word, has always required submission to his supreme authority from both Christians and

---

[6] God's sovereignty is supreme power and a freedom from external control. No one counsels God as to how he should be, what he should do or how he should act. Sovereignty is fundamentally the supremacy of God, the kingship of God, and the godhood of God. The sovereignty of the God of Scripture is absolute, irresistible, and infinite in power. The Bible states that God is sovereign over the entire universe, (Psa. 103:19; Rom 8:28; Eph. 1:11), over all of nature, (Psa. 135:6-7; Matt. 5:45; 6:25-30), over angels and Satan, (Psa. 103:20-21; Job 1:12), over nations, (Psa. 47:7-9; Dan. 2:20-21; 4:34-35), over human beings, (1 Sam. 2:6-7; Gal. 1:15-16), over animals, (Psa. 104:21-30; 1 Kings 17:4-6), over things that seem to be an accident, (Prov. 16:33; John 1:7; Matt. 10:29), over free acts of men, (Exod. 3:21; 12:25-36; Ezek. 7:27), over sinful acts of men and Satan, (2 Sam. 24:1; 1 Chron. 21:1; Gen 45:5; 50:20).

unbelievers. "Submit yourselves therefore to God," (James 4:7). "Say to God, "How awesome are Your works! Through the greatness of Your power Your enemies shall submit themselves to You," (Psa. 66:3). God is *over all*. "But our God is in the heavens: he hath done whatsoever he hath pleased," (Psa. 115:3). The same word used to describe Nehemiah's work, is the word ascribing *greatness* to God. Deut. 10:17," For the LORD your God is God of gods, and Lord of lords, a great God, a mighty, and a terrible, which regardeth not persons, nor taketh reward." Psalm 95:3, "For the LORD is a great God, and a great King above all gods."

God is great and his Messiah is great. His Messiah is great because the Messiah *is God*. Titus 2:13, "Looking for that blessed hope, and the glorious appearing of the great God and our Saviour Jesus Christ." God reigns supreme in his Kingdom. He is infinitely greater in dominion and power than anything. He is the Most High God, the Lord of heaven and earth. God is supreme essence, supreme goodness, supreme truth and supreme beauty. Supreme in every respect. Everything submits (or will submit at the throne of Christ) itself to God, whether in this life or the life to come. God rules *all* creation. God rules all men. God rules all angelic beings. God rules all devils. God rules...PERIOD. God rules over the king in order to change his heart to send Nehemiah to build the wall. "The king's heart is in the hand of the LORD, as the rivers of water: he turneth it whithersoever he will,"

(Prov. 21:1). Consider that such a statement is drawn merely from a proverb, and proverbs are wisdom sayings, or sayings of *common sense*. One common sense understanding in this is that, "God rules."

As God is great, all of God's *works* are great, both in his governing, and through his Messiah as it regard sin and salvation. Since Christ's work is great, being God's Messiah, that induces Christians to imitate him.[7] Consider, then, the work of Christ. His incarnation is great. He took on the necessary form to uphold the covenant of redemption in becoming fully man. He did this without sin, being in perfect conformity to the Law of God; fulfilling it perfectly. Christ "...was in all points tempted like as we are, yet without sin," (Heb. 4:15). He sacrificially laid down his life for his friends, his sheep, his church, in atoning for them and saving them. He took their sins. He took God's wrath. Yes, "...even Jesus, which delivered us from the wrath to come," (1 Thess. 1:10). Like Nehemiah, Jesus was beckoned to come down off the cross by his enemies, *by the devil*. "Save Yourself, and come down from the cross!" (Mark 15:30). The greatest temptation of all time given to him was to come down. Come down and stop the work, physically morally, and covenantally. Come down and cease the work. Come down and give up this resolve to save men. Come down and stop the means by which men may

---

[7] "Be ye therefore followers of God, as dear children; and walk in love, as Christ also hath loved us, and hath given himself for us an offering and a sacrifice to God for a sweetsmelling savour," (Eph. 5:1-2).

come and worship the Father. Come down and show that you are not God's Fellow, not God's Redeemer, not man's Savior.

Yet, being God's Son, Christ's resolution was consigned to the terrors of the cross. He would not have any gall, no anesthetic to cloud his mind, no coming down, he was about a great work and he could not come down lest the work cease. "Why should the work cease while I come down to you? I am about a great work. I am about the greatest work in all creation. Who are you to even suggest that God's great work of redemption stop? I will not come down. I am committed to the Father, by joy, and will endure this cross." Resolved, Christ remained nailed to the cross and was crucified, died and was buried, being forsaken of the Father for the sins of his people as a substitutionary sacrifice.

Christ's resurrection and ascension were also great. After three days he was raised from the dead and ascended into heaven, "which He worked in Christ when he raised him from the dead and seated him at his right hand in the heavenly places," (Eph. 1:20). Raised from the dead as a stamp of approval on his great work, he ascended to heaven, having gone there to work other great works for all believers. He went there to open up, as it were, the gates of heaven. That is a *great work indeed.* He goes there to prepare a place for his people (John 14:3). That is a great work indeed. He goes there to take possession of it, and in the meantime to intercede for them by his Spirit. His intercession is a great work.

Mark 1: Resolved to Do Great Works for the Glory of God

He now sits in all glory at the right hand of the Father,[8] interceding on behalf of his people in this great work of redemption that never ends. He sends the Spirit of grace to his people from the throne of God (John 15:26). This is also a great work of his intercession. He stands between the Father and his people in constant view to turn away any judgment on his saints. This is a great work. He deposits assurance from such intercession into the hearts of his people who look to him by faith. This is a great work. In this he is, "our stepping stone to heaven." This is a *very great* work he does. And, in the end, Christ's judgment will be great as well. He shall return again in judgment to crush his enemies, restore creation and save his people in ushering them into a final consummation of eternal bliss. His people will not be judged with condemnation – no, there is *no condemnation* in this great work he accomplishes on behalf of his people (Rom. 8:1). In fact, they will even *enter into* this great work of judgment with him, as he judges the nations. "Do you not know that the saints will judge the world?" (1 Cor. 6:2). All this work, all this merit, all this redeeming by Christ is a very *very* great work; an *infinitely* great work.

    The greatness of God and the work of the Lord Jesus Christ ought to be motivating influences for every Christian to be about the work God has called them to in living righteously before him. All God commands them as the Great King is a great work that they are to

---

[8] Heb. 1:3, 8:1, 10:12, 12:2.

live for. Living before the face of God *is* a great work. It is to order every aspect of life in submission to the great God, and to gain the resolute contending for holiness that Christ had.[9]

Living before God is not a compartmentalized thing, as if God and Christ only have to do with a short time in church on the Lord's Day. Rather, such work centers on the saint's direction to glorify God in *all things*. "Therefore, whether you eat or drink, or whatever you do, do all to the glory of God," (1 Cor. 10:31). All living, in every facet of the Christian life, is set before the face of God's supreme eye and requires every Christian to submit to King Jesus' sovereignty in everything.[10] All of life for the Christian, then, is a great work. *God* counts it as a great work. Nehemiah saw building a wall as a great work because God was its author.

The second point to consider is: sin is always striving to *hinder* the great work of being a Christian. Where Christians strive towards the goal, "to the

---

[9] William Ames said, "Theology is doctrine or teaching of living to God." Peter van Mastricht further edits this and said, "Theology is doctrine or teaching of living to God through Christ." In expounding this I will take this one step further. "Theology is doctrine or teaching of living to God through Christ in the power of walking in the Spirit." See my work, *Walking Victoriously in the Power of the Spirit* for a full discussion of this.

[10] "Theology is a divine doctrine by the Scriptures, of religious living to God in order to man's happiness and God's glory," Francis Roberts (1609–1675) said. McMahon, C. Matthew, *Light from Old Paths: An Anthology of Puritan Quotations,* Vol. 1, (Coconut Creek, FL: Puritan Publications, 2014), section on Doctrine.

upwards call in Christ," sin desires to pull Christians away from Christ – to pull them down off the wall! Whenever some true religious duty is at hand, sin comes to pull the Christian *down, down, down* off the wall. The world, the flesh and the devil are out to kill... (Rom. 6:23), such wages and working are of *death*. Sin crouches and waits for the prime opportunity to master the Christian (Gen. 4:7). It tries to revive the old man at every opportunity, calling the Christian into the plains of Ono, far away from his duty, far away from him who was crucified for them, and it takes that opportunity to *master* Christians, instead of Christians mastering sin (Psalm 19:13). The Apostle says, Rom. 6:12, "Therefore do not let sin reign (*i.e. exercise its power*) in your mortal body, that you should obey it in its lusts." Nehemiah sent a message to his enemies. "I am doing a great work, so that I cannot come down: why should the work cease, while I leave it, and come down to you?" He sent the message each time in the same way. The Christian must send a similar message when sin raises its ugly head. The Christian ought always to "tell sin" about the great work he is about until sin gets sick and tired of hearing it. Sin comes *often* as the enemies did to the wall, with the same message. Sanballat came four times. Sin's message is always the same.[11] Sin says, "I'm fun for a season (Heb. 11:25). I will give you satisfaction. I will fulfill all your

---

[11] "And it came to pass, as she spake to Joseph *day by day,* that he hearkened not unto her, to lie by her, or to be with her," (Gen. 39:10). See my work, *Joseph's Resolve: The Unreasonableness of Sinning Against God* for a full study on that verse.

desires." Sin can never fulfill man's desires; not in a real, holy, righteous and eternal sense. Not even in a temporary sense. It may be considered as *fun for a season*, but the cloaked ending to that story is death and hell. Its wages are unbearable, filled with those who weep and gnash their teeth under divine wrath. Sin is diametrically opposed to the great work of upholding the Moral Law of God to both love God and love one's neighbor. The imagery of Nehemiah's work and the wall, the work of God and the Christian coming down off the wall, is all one and the same. Christians are beckoned minute after minute to cease working for God by the world, flesh and devil. They work tirelessly to pull them away from the work. "Put down your sword. Put down your trowel. Put down God's work," they cry out.

Sin transforms a Christian's great work for God into *great sin* against God. From love of the great God to a great love of the *self*. It is a "great" sin to stop acting like a Christian because God is great, and the people of God are to be reflecting his holy nature. When the Christian sins he sins greater than the devil. When the Christian sins against the Lord of glory, when it is a sin against the Lord Christ, it is as if he builds scaffolding in front of the cross, climbs up, looks Christ in the face for a moment. ...and spits in his face while he hangs there. At least the centurions who crucified him did it *before* he was hanging on the cross. The Christian does it with a metaphorical ladder to climb up into heaven to spit in the face of Christ seated on the throne of glory. It is like trampling on the pool of blood at the foot of the cross and walking away. Devils don't sin against Christ's blood, only Christians do.[12]

The world, the flesh and the devil are in opposition to any great work the Christian engages in. The world offers *Pilgrim's Progress'* picture of *Vanity Fair* and all its wares. It says to the Christian "You don't need to pray so much. You don't need to lead your families so much. You don't need to read your bible so much. You don't need to meditate on the word daily so much. You don't need to reach out to others for the Gospel's sake so much." Rather, they desire Christians to be lazy – a little folding of the hands to sleep. "Take a break...come down, don't be so obsessive about it." Nehemiah worked with a sword in one hand and a trowel in the other. The world, the flesh and the devil hide the hook of temptation to draw the Christian away from God's greatness in the bait of opposition and rebellion, and the task of being a great Christian before God's face is always assaulted day to day.

Where are all the *great* Christians doing *great* work? The flesh wars against the Spirit, (Gal. 5:16-17), Paul exhorts. Where are the battle-ready Christians, the great fighters, the great workers, the great resolutions for God's glory? This life is a war. Christians are involved in a war 24-hours a day and ought to stand firm and resolved with that sword and trowel because their work

---

[12] "How then can I do this great wickedness, and sin against God?" (Gen. 39:9).

is a great work...because sin is always trying to hinder the great work of *being* a Christian.

The third point to consider is that: Christians are never to cease the great work they are about, no matter what. It would be better to suffer the greatest affliction than to commit the least sin against God. To cease the work that God has given the Christian of living a righteous life before him would be to shipwreck their faith.[13] If the Christian ceases his duties, the work stops. The Christian runs the race in order to win the prize, not simply to finish the race. "Know ye not that they which run in a race run all, but one receiveth the prize? So run, that ye may obtain," (1 Cor. 9:24). In this there is a great urgency and determination about *living the life* of a Christian. Was Nehemiah determined? Was he urgent? Was he *resolved?*

Great works require *great resolve*. It was a great charge for the people with great opposition, but they were glad to have the sword and trowel used together for God's glory. They worked, and if needs be, they would have fought. No doubt there was difficulty in that, or maybe some level of inconvenience. But they had a resolved mind to the work. The way to heaven is by work and conflict every step of the way, until the Christian gets to heaven.[14] They are resolved to hold steadfastly to Jesus Christ, imitating his great work in

---

[13] "...which some having put away concerning faith have made shipwreck," (1 Tim. 1:19).
[14] "...since that time the kingdom of God is preached, and every man presseth into it," (Luke 16:16).

obedience and submission to God, with a full purpose of heart, no matter what it costs them. Thomas Manton said, "We make no great work in religion until we so mind these things that we come to such a resolution as Paul had, "And when he would not be persuaded, we ceased, saying, The will of the Lord be done." (Acts 21:1).[15] Paul meant, I am prepared, I am ready, not only to be bound, but to die at Jerusalem for the sake of the Lord Jesus Christ. Such a resolution should be in minding all the great works that the Christian does before God.

All duties accomplished for God and Christ are a great work for the Christian. Sin is always trying to hinder the great work of being a Christian. Christians are never to cease the great work they are about, *no matter what.*

If you are a professing believer, you are to be about great works for God as a Christian. Every Christian duty accomplished for Christ is a great work. Consider your devotional life: it is a *great* work. If your devotional life consists of less than five minutes a day with God, *you don't have a devotional life.* You have not yet started your devotional life. The Christian life is not even a work for you because you *have yet to engage in it.* Work is *work.* Is your devotional life work? A basic devotional life should consist in three parts: 1) Reading and studying the word of God. "This Book of the Law shall not depart from your mouth, but you shall meditate

---

[15] Manton, Thomas, *The Complete Works of Thomas Manton*, Vol. 11 (London: James Nisbet & Co., 1873), 446.

in it day and night, that you may observe to do according to all that is written in it. For then you will make your way prosperous, and then you will have good success," (Jos. 1:8). To accomplish a great work, much relies on this reading and studying. 2) Godly meditation of the word. "But his delight is in the law of the LORD, And in His law he meditates day and night," (Psa. 1:2). This is another great work of being in that constant form of "considering what God teaches you" in your bible reading which extends out to godly meditation. And, 3) prayer. "…pray without ceasing." Do you see the significance of these commanded duties? The word not departing from your mouth, meditating day and night, praying without ceasing. Such commands are given by our great King and are *great* works. If Joshua 1:8-9, Psalm 1:2 and 1 Thessalonians 5:17 were the only three Scriptures in all the Bible that direct Christians to pray, read, and ponder through God's word, they would be enough. Luther said, "Work, work from early until late. In fact, I have so much to do that I shall spend the first three hours in prayer."[16] Great Christians have great works they do before God. Great works start with great *piety* before God. Without your devotions to God there is *no* devotion to God. Nehemiah's desire was to be back

---

[16] Gilchrist Lawson, James, *Cyclopedia of Religious Anecdotes*, (1923) 303, compiled by James Gilchrist Lawson. In context it reads fully: "Work, work from early until late. In fact, I have so much to do that I shall spend the first three hours in prayer." Luther said this when responding to a question about what his plans for the day were.

in the temple worshipping God and he began with prayer and fasting. "I was fasting and praying before the God of heaven," (Neh. 1:4). That turned into traveling, governing, building, and fighting if needs be, all with *resolve*.

Consider your family life as a great work. The training of your children and their family worship is a great work. Is your family known for its godliness and piety? Consider your personal work as a great work, being a *religious tradesman*. Mothers taking care of their children, businessmen and all concerns for the workplace, kids learning in school, students in the pursuit of their vocation, *etc.* are all tasks that you even might think are menial. But all these are great works. All of it tends towards the glory of God for the Christian.

Consider your church life as a great work. This involves attending worship, gathering together to worship, gathering together to pray, and to have fellowship. It includes ministering to the body and ministering to one another. These are all *great* works. They are all *very great works* because they are all commanded of God and motioned by the Spirit of Christ. Yes, they are *very important* works. Exercising your gifts among others in church is a great and most important work for the good of the body of Christ.[17] Imagine your hand not desiring to be used all of a sudden? Or your leg decides it's not going to work

---

[17] "So we, being many, are one body in Christ, and every one members one of another," (Rom. 12:5).

anymore. Together the church is the body of Christ and *each one of you is a part of its great work.* Some are hands, some are eyes, some are legs and such. All this work that each member exercises is a great work. In all the Christian duties that could be performed, you are required by God not to abandon your post as a good solder in Christ's army! Cease your work? No. Stop? Absolutely not. Your response should consistently be, "I am about a great work, how can I come down and the work cease?" I am about prayer. I am about study. I am about praise and adoration. I am about worship. I am about nurturing others. I am about contending for the faith once delivered to me. I am about eating and drinking and all things for God's glory as if it they are all great works.

It is a sad reality that being resolute for Christ is a waxing and waning issue. Christians *excuse* themselves from great works too often. Doubt, unskilled, inability, lack of strength, no time, differing theological ideas and views, all play a part in this. You might even say, "I'm not like Nehemiah," and use that as an excuse not to do more in the body of Christ. Really? *Nehemiah was a cup bearer.* He brought a drink from here to there, (Neh. 1:11). But the moment God motioned the work in his heart, he was a man of resolve and in no way would the work cease for him. If we would imitate such a resolve, we would accomplish such works with the sword in one hand and the trowel in the other. Did Nehemiah suddenly by osmosis learn all these things?

Was he *zapped* by the Spirit to suddenly know how construction works? How to build a wall? How to be a governor of the people? No, no, he had to learn these things, but he was utterly *resolved to do it*. The Christian is never to be about *excuses*, but about great works for King Jesus.

If God's greatness in commanding us to duty is not enough to prompt you to consider all that you do as a great work, is not Christ's sacrifice enough of a motivation for you? *He died for you.* You are not your own. "For ye are bought with a price: therefore glorify God in your body, and in your spirit, which are God's," (1 Cor. 6:20). You are commissioned to do a great work for King Jesus. 1 Cor. 15:58 says, "Therefore, my beloved brethren, be ye steadfast, unmovable, always abounding in the work of the Lord, forasmuch as ye know that your labor is not in vain in the Lord." Yes, the apostle said, "always" abounding in the work of the Lord. This is because, Nehemiah 6:3, "I am doing *a great work*, so that I cannot come down: why should the work cease, whilst I leave it, and come down to you?" You are doing the work, not *talking* about the work. "Doing" a great work is resolved to accomplish it by exercising everything that would be required to do it. And then, faithfulness in the work will lead to verse 16b, "...this work was done by our God." The Spirit of God works in and through you for his good pleasure, and at the end of your earthly travail you will be able to give all glory to Christ and will say too, "this work was done by our God." But be resolved to know that God never does a work in you *without you.* You will have to say to the Lord, "I resolved never to come down Lord. I was resolved never to cease the work. I resolved always to do a great work for God." Every temptation that draws us away from our duty, should hasten us toward a firmer resolution for success. If all of this seems foreign to you, and you do not think about living righteously before God in this way, it may very well be that you are not yet a Christian.

Consider those who are not Christians. This text in Nehemiah *screams at them.* They are opposed to the great work of *being* a Christian. Sanballat, Tobiah and the others were hecklers metaphorically standing at the foot of the wall, trying to drag people down off the wall into hell where they were going. They opposed God himself in doing so. "And it happened, when all our enemies heard of it, and all the nations around us saw these things, that they were very disheartened in their own eyes; for they perceived that this work was done by our God," (Neh. 6:16). To be *opposed to the work* is to be *against* the work. Jesus said "he who is not for me is against me," (Matthew 12:30). They might think, "Well, I'm for Christ, I'm not *hostile* to him, I just don't do those things which Christians are supposed to do *all the time."* No, Jesus says that such people are *against* the work. That is Christ's assessment. "He who is not for me is against me. He who does not gather with me scatters." The Christian life is never merely about intention, but involves action. "Blessed are they that hear the word of God, *and keep it*," (Luke 11:28).

You must have an interest in Christ, and an interest in God's work, and then God will give you an interest in *doing* a great work for him. If you sit where you are and do nothing, you show yourself to be the Sanballats and Tobiahs of the world. What do you think Sanballat, Tobiah and Geshem are thinking *right now?* You do not want to be in their shoes in hell. What is Judas thinking right now in hell? Along with the disciples, Judas did many *great works*. Judas heard all of Christ's sermons. Judas preached. Judas helped the poor. Yes, he did many great works indeed. But he did them as a hypocrite, which turned those works against him. There are great works to be done, they can only be accomplished in Christ, and through Christ, where Judas did neither of those. "Herein is my Father glorified, that ye bear much fruit; so shall ye be my disciples. As the Father hath loved me, so have I loved you: continue ye in my love. If ye keep my commandments, ye shall abide in my love," (John 15:8-10).

There is also a word to be said to the gospel hypocrite. A *hypocrite* is one who "thinks" he is about a great work but is really not. He pretends to get into heaven, but doesn't. Such people are pretenders (the meaning of the Greek *hupocrites*) in the church. They *think* they are on the wall, or at least in the company of those working for God, but they are truly not. These are people who have gotten their foot on the first or second wrung of the ladder to consider it, or at the very least to seem as though they are part of the *ministry crowd*. They say: sometimes I pray, sometimes I read the word, sometimes I come to church, sometimes I fellowship, sometimes I say something about the Bible, sometimes I help out. They do enough in all these things to keep their conscience *somewhat* settled and give the appearance of godliness, but deny its transforming power. "Having a form of godliness, but denying the power thereof: from such turn away," (2 Tim. 3:5).

You do not want to be one a hypocrite. These people are really onlookers to the work being done; a talker – they talk about the work, but are never really "doing" the work. It is interesting to note that the *elders* in Judah were not scolded by Sanballat and the others, only Nehemiah was scolded because he was *doing* the work. The others were simply self-deceived, *doing nothing*. And yet they forgot, "The Lord knows the heart..."

There is a strong delusion and deception for such people if they fall into this hypocritical way and remain in it. The bible calls it *ignorance*.[18] They are ignorant of what God actually requires. The character, Ignorance, in *Pilgrim's Progress* was thrown into hell. Keep in mind though, he made it all the way to the gate of heaven. Bunyan says, "And I saw that the mouth of hell was even

---

[18] "...sin through ignorance," (Lev. 4:2). "Having the understanding darkened, being alienated from the life of God through the ignorance that is in them, because of the blindness of their heart," (Eph. 4:18).

there at the gate of heaven." Hell is there, right at the gate, at the judgment seat of Christ in the end. Ignorance will be thrown into hell every time.

And these enemies were *among* the people of God. They were not on the side in which God was working in them, because they were not about a great work *for* him. "And it happened, when all our enemies heard of it, and all the nations around us saw these things, that they were very disheartened in their own eyes; for they perceived that this work was done by our God," (Neh. 6:16).

May we all be steadfastly resolved to say of our Christian life and walk, in considering the great God whom we serve, and the Lord of glory, King Jesus, whom we are to imitate, "I am doing a great work, so that I cannot come down: why should the work cease, while I leave it, and come down to you?"

MARK 2: Resolved to Contend for the Faith

Jude 1:3, "Beloved, while I was very diligent to write to you concerning our common salvation, I found it necessary to write to you exhorting you to contend earnestly for the faith which was once for all delivered to the saints."

The epistle of Jude is a general epistle to the church, taking up the besiege of false doctrine in the church, and the need to overcome it. The writer is Jude, his name coming from *Judah*, possibly *Thaddaeus*, or typically *Judas*, but this is not Judas Iscariot. His office is written as, "a servant of Jesus Christ." This is in direct relation to his apostleship. The Apostle "Judas (not Iscariot) said to Him, "Lord, how is it that You will manifest Yourself to us, and not to the world?" (John 14:22-23). He is designated, "the brother of James." He is differentiated in Scripture from Judas the traitor, the son of perdition. Jude, the author of this one-chapter epistle, which the Scriptures describe *as an apostle*, is in personal relation to James. Matthew 13:55, "Is not this the carpenter's son? is not his mother called Mary? and his brethren, James, and Joses, and Simon, and Judas?" (compare also Mark 6:3). Jude does not assume some superiority in filial relation to the Lord Jesus Christ. Instead, he merely mentions he is brother of James in a humble fashion.

Jude's desire in writing this epistle is given as a letter to those close to His heart. "Beloved," His concern was for the *beloved brethren,* those loved of God. In Scripture, this word is used of those who have a very intense love, a dear and tender love for others. These are very special people indeed, who are sanctified by God the Father, kept (preserved) by Jesus Christ, and showered with mercy, peace and love which is hoped to be in great abundance.

He says, "while I was very diligent to write to you concerning our common salvation..." He longed to write about the common salvation that he shared with Jesus and the church. "If anyone loves Me, he will keep My word; and My Father will love him, and We will come to him and make Our home with him," Jesus says. Jude gave himself to a "diligence" of intention in this same vein. The Reformers used this term for, "an earnest intention of the mind." It included carefulness, forward movement, speed, and earnest care in being resolved for God in such things.

Jude's desire was of diligence, with spiritual blessing, and hoped he could have simply enjoyed writing a letter on the work of Christ in his life and for the benefit of their new-found life in the Lord. The exceptional subject of his desire to write was on the common salvation, its blessedness, its origin, its Surety, its Redeemer, justification, sanctification, covenant, the work of God in the Kingdom of God in all its vast array. There are various topics that could have been taken up by his diligent pen. Yet, in considering everything to be considered in writing this short epistle, for the good of the church, Jude says, "I found it necessary to write…" This particular phrase takes on itself the urgency of obligation. He had to do this at once and could not prepare this letter at his own leisure. The ease was gone, speed was necessary, and there is a fire about his words. This letter could not have been written any faster than Jude could have penned it. It was imperative that he write it and send this letter out to those he loved, to those called of God in the church, to those who partook of this common salvation. The people needed to receive it and read it because of its great importance, its necessity. He was not able to be present, and in his absence, he wrote to them with all urgency.

This short epistle, a one-chapter letter, was vitally significant for the strengthening of the church. Through Jude, God gives his church the constant, standing rule of a written word, in order to show the preparation needed to cleave to Christ in truth, to be resolved in it without wavering. It was also *necessary* that God would have an apostle write it, because Jude is a *messenger from God*, officiating as an elder, as an apostle, over the good of the church. What was his urgent message?

Jude says, "Exhorting you…" The way the epistle is written is by way of doctrine, command and exhortation. The word "exhort" is used in various ways in Scripture based on its context. Sometimes it is used to implore, Matt 8:5, "There came to him a centurion, beseeching him." Sometimes it signifies to comfort and encourage, as 2 Cor. 7:6, "And we were comforted by the coming of Titus." Sometimes it signifies to exhort, Heb. 3:13, "Exhort one another daily," as it is here in Jude.

What was this exhortation? "...to contend earnestly." This type of urging was to encourage or beseech someone to some task. The phrase is actually one Greek word, commonly used by military leaders as a word to employ a fearless soldier who goes into the battlefield. Our English word is translated to mean, "great effort and exertion." In extra biblical literature, it was used of athletes who contended or struggled during their games to win at any physical cost. It is only used here in Jude in the New Testament. It conveys a seriousness surrounding the ground of contention. In some way there is a significant enemy that must be stopped. It is not going to come easy. There will be significant stamina needed to defeat such an enemy; great *resolve* surrounding a great work for God. There is no truth of God which is recovered out of the hands of the devil without great wrestling and bloodshed. It is going to require all their stamina and all their strength. And the strength expended has to be done in such a way in order to gain a real victory over this enemy.

Jude says that this contending and resolve is, "for the faith which was once for all delivered to the saints." What is "the faith?" It can be many things from Scripture. Sound doctrine, "The devils believe," (James

2:19). It can refer to fleeting faith, "who believe for a while and in time of temptation fall away," (Luke 8:13). It can refer to justifying faith, which is biblical and relies on the promises of Christ, for salvation and remission of sin by Christ's imputed righteousness. "But to him who does not work but believes on Him who justifies the ungodly, his faith is accounted for righteousness," (Rom. 4:5). There is also in Scripture examples of a profession of faith. "Your faith is spoken of throughout the world," (Rom. 1:8).

However, here in Jude it is used for the great body of *the doctrine of faith*, or *the whole body of truth to be believed about the salvation one may have in Jesus Christ*. It is the entire body of Christian doctrine believed and given "once delivered," that Christians are to uphold against any false doctrine or adversaries that rise up against God's truth. Only this "body of faith" leads to eternal life. Only the entirety of this singular truth delivered once is what is historically defined as, "the rule of faith." This is what is to be believed and applied throughout the history of the Christian church in connection with Christ and his work of redemption. Jesus Christ imparts to all believers, all the spiritual blessings that he merits, and withholds nothing from his children, from any that have union with him, in this body of doctrine.[19] The faith which has been delivered to

---

[19] "And they continued steadfastly in the apostles' doctrine and fellowship, and in breaking of bread, and in prayers," (Acts 2:42). "...and if there be any other thing that is contrary to sound doctrine; according to the glorious gospel of the blessed God, which was

the church can be nothing but the system of doctrine contained in divine revelation. This is the *faith* once delivered. The church is called even to suffer for the foundation of Christ's house; this faith once delivered to the saints, which is the common salvation, which everything stands upon. For this, all Christians are to earnestly contend (Jude verse 3), for this they strive together (Phil. 1:27); they are resolved in it. Truths are often denied, shunned, and *resolved against* and such warping of the truth ruins the church with a rottenness that is almost irreversible and uncorrectable when it starts. The Apostle Paul called false doctrine "gangrene" or a "canker".[20] These are deviations to accepted Christian truth, breaches in fundamental doctrines infiltrated into the church, allowed to fester there, where such changes to truth are either nearer to the foundation or at a greater distance from it. The closer they are to the foundation of essential Christian belief, the more dangerous they are. It is better to have a breach at the top of a building, than at its foundation, because if the foundation is rotten, the whole building will fall.

The faith that Jude speaks of is "once delivered" which shows the total insufficiency of man to find out

---

committed to my trust," (1 Tim. 1:10-11). "Till I come, give attendance to reading, to exhortation, to doctrine," (1 Tim. 4:13). "He that abideth in the doctrine of Christ, he hath both the Father and the Son," (2 John 1:9).

[20] "And their word will eat as doth a canker: of whom is Hymenaeus and Philetus; Who concerning the truth have erred, saying that the resurrection is past already; and overthrow the faith of some," (2 Tim. 2:17-18).

this body of faith by himself. Everything delivered to these Christians embodies the faith, once given, and it contains in it the will of God in the redemption of Jesus Christ. It is no small matter. It focuses on Christ – the Messiah of God, the Kingdom of God, the incarnation of the Son of God, expiation of sin by his death, justification by faith, sanctification by the Spirit, the covenants of God, *everything*. None of this could have ever been discovered by man unless God had revealed it to them – specially revealed, in special revelation. It is not a faith created by the saints, but given *to* the saints, *delivered to them*. It is not something to be found of one's self. It must be given by God. Here the Christian must admire the great glory and work of the Redeemer in the Covenant of Redemption and the work that Christ does to seek and save that which is lost. Thomas Manton said that this faith is, "delivered, not invented."[21] It is never fabricated or part of some human imagination. God *delivered* his heart to his saints in this word. It was written down for his people to know, that there would be no mistaking what his desire is for the church. "These things have I written unto you that believe on the name of the Son of God; that ye may know that ye have eternal life, and that ye may believe on the name of the Son of God," (1 John 5:13).

  Consider who this *faith* is given to. It is not given to everyone, but to the saints; once for all entrusted to

---

[21] Manton, Thomas, *The Complete Works of Thomas Manton*, Vol. 5, (London: James Nisbet & Co., 1871), 106.

them. Such truth is "entrusted to the saints" like a family heirloom. Literally, it was handed down to them by divine condescension. God stooped down to deliver the truth of the Messiah in a body of doctrine called "the faith," to his saints which explains everything they need to know about God's Kingdom and God's King. Jude demonstrates the vital urgency of guarding and keeping this body of truth which has been graciously given to the saints, by God himself. That ought to be one of the chief motives for these Christians to hear Jude's exhortation. God has entrusted something to the church, and it is the church's job to contend for it, even unto death, resolved to contend for it for all time. These saints receive the truth because, as Christ says, "My sheep hear my voice."[22] Jude's appeal is for the church to be theologically literate, to be those guarding the valuables of Christ. These Christians, by Jude's command, take the objective standard of God's rule of faith which he has entrusted to them and contend earnestly for it as if their lives depend on it. And, yes, the spiritual good of their lives do depend on it. So, they are resolved in this even if it costs them everything.

 The doctrine to consider here is that: the saints of God are divinely commanded, by necessity, to be resolved to contend for the faith in proclaiming it and preserving it, no matter what.

---

[22] "My sheep hear my voice, and I know them, and they follow me," (John 10:27).

There are many who are ready to corrupt the church either for overthrowing religion, or for convenience to pacify them. The devil is happy with either. He will have churches overthrown in their faith succumbing to all kinds of false teaching, and gather up people more quickly for hell in that way. Or, he is happy if the faith, the truth, is subverted on key doctrines to weaken the church, that it might not be more militant, confident, resolved, assured and the like, against his onslaughts. Subvert the truth, and the effective work of the church is weakened. By way of "Christian convenience" where people don't really care about the truth, subverting the truth lessens its importance. More people are attracted to natural religion, a religion based on things *they do* to make themselves *feel better,* and so key, fundamental doctrines, are seen as "minor issues." The faith of the church then becomes a matter of taste and preference. It is an emphasis on what is enjoyed, or more accepted by their mere pleasure, rather than holding and contending for that faith at all costs. This was *not* Jude's position on the faith once delivered to the saints.

The saints, in battling against indifference, are to be resolved contenders for God. Every Christian should do this, and none are exempt. This is not a verse merely for pastors. This is not a verse merely for theologians. The *saints* are entrusted with this. William Jenkyn, who wrote an extraordinary commentary on Jude said,

"Every child of wisdom should justify their parent."[23] In other words, all Christians are required to contend for the faith in life and doctrine.

The saints must contend for the truth of the gospel in various ways. Here are four ways saints can do this. 1) By praying for the success of the Gospel Ministry. Not only in their own church, but in all of Christendom. In the seminaries where pastors are taught, that they would be delivered from error, guarded against it. Praying that God would raise up godly and learned ministers, powerful preachers, eminent in piety the likes of which rival the heroes of church history. Praying for the people of their church that they would all hold to the truth once delivered, and not waiver. Just because the Christian does not physically meet with some heretic on the road, does not mean that they do not have an effect on the kingdom and its use of the truth, or give up being a contender. Prayer is a great means that God uses to defeat his enemies in the kingdom of darkness. But the Christian has to pray and pull-down strongholds. Prayer, in this way, is vitally linked to God's decrees and providence, if one exercises that and practices it.

2) By the conduct of their lives. The Christian's conversation, or the way they walk and talk and act, must be the conversation of heaven. "...that you may become blameless and harmless, children of God without fault in the midst of a crooked and perverse

---

[23] Jenkyn, William, *An Exposition of the Epistle of Jude*, (London: Samuel Holdsworth, 1839) 71.

generation, among whom you shine as lights in the world," (Phil. 2:15). "Let your light so shine before men," (Matt. 5:16). The Christian is to walk according to the faith once delivered. This means the Christian must *know* what that faith is; that body of doctrine, and those truths, without which, they cannot walk, and cannot be imitators of God, much less contend for the faith, which they are *commanded* to do. They must live out the testimony of their baptism.[24] Their lives are living sermons to others; where they are exhorting one another while it is still called today. Christians must, "speak often one to another," Mal. 3:16; Heb.10:24, to spur one another onto good works, to encourage one another. By speaking to one another without fear that they will in some way offend another brother or sister even if they are holding steadfastly to the Word of God. God uses the word to wash us and the Holy Spirit uses other Christians to do just that. By openly speaking about the truth. "But sanctify the Lord God in your hearts, and always be ready to give a defense to everyone who asks you a reason for the hope that is in you, with meekness and fear; having a good conscience, that when they defame you as evildoers, those who revile your good conduct in Christ may be ashamed," (1 Peter 3:15-16).

---

[24] "The public administration of baptism, he not only judged most agreeable to the nature and end of the ordinance, but found to be very profitable and edifying to the congregation; for he always took that occasion, not only to explain the nature of the ordinance, but affectionately and pathetically to excite people duly to improve their baptism." Henry, Matthew, *An Account of the Life and Death of Mr. Philip Henry*, (London: 1698), 177–178.

Mark 2: Resolved to Contend for the Faith

Many Christians cannot speak a word of instruction and comfort to others, but spend the time they have with other saints, often, in silence. Or, that they say things of little to no effect such as, "Be well, and I hope you are comforted. I'll pray for you." What good is that? The saints cannot afford to live in ignorance of God's word, or because they wrongly think that the whole burden of this duty of exhorting another person lies on the shoulders of the minister.

I might make a brief note here, that some Christians may even be called to suffer for the faith in contending for it. William Jenkyn said, "He that saves his life, and forsakes the faith, never lived comfortably; but thousands that have lost their lives, and kept the faith, have died joyfully. How honorable is it to follow our Captain through mud and blood!"[25]

Now, in order for the saints to fulfill this divine command, they must *know* the Bible. What do Christians commonly think of when they picture a theologian? An old man sitting at his desk, covered in a layer of dust which fell upon him from some ancient books which he had been pulling off the shelf. It is unfortunate that Christians often reserve this conception of a theologian for that select few. That imagery is not generally what a theologian is. The word *theology* itself means to *have a word about God.* The saints should have *many* words about the faith once

---

[25] Ibid.

delivered to them. They are in fact to *contend* for it. There is no time to be silent if they are to be useful.

The directive posed by Jude in this verse, says, "Christians are *contenders* for the faith," which is the same as saying, they are resolved and informed theologians. They are commanded to be theologically literate. How could they contend for anything without being fit to that purpose? How can a boxer contend for the championship of the world if he is not trained and ready? Jude did not say *some of the truth*, not *a piece of the truth*, but *all of the truth* that God has declared in his word is the place where the "Christian contender" fights. This is a difficult task and weighty burden for most Christians because it implies *earnest study*. "Study to show yourself approved..." (2 Timothy 2:15). Is this only for the minister? "These were more fair-minded than those in Thessalonica, in that they received the word with all readiness, and searched the Scriptures daily to find out whether these things were so," (Act. 17:11). No, it is the task of the resolute saint to be studious in the things of God.

Jude even tells his readers why he wants them to contend for the faith... "For certain men...." (verse 4) exchange the truth of God for a lie. This requires Christians to love the truth. "The coming of the lawless one is according to the working of Satan, with all power, signs, and lying wonders, and with all unrighteous deception among those who perish, because they did not receive the love of the truth, that they might be saved,"

Mark 2: Resolved to Contend for the Faith

(2 Thess. 2:9-10). Loving the truth is the same as loving God. Being a good theologian, then, is something intrinsically linked to being a lover of truth. "Keep yourselves in the love of God, looking for the mercy of our Lord Jesus Christ unto eternal life." Who said that? Who said to keep yourselves in the love of God in that way; it was Jude, in verse 21. Loving the truth turns the Christian on into becoming a *contender* so they can do two things: 1) they present this truth in their present day. It is for *now*. It is not hidden away. It is taken out and shared, and talked about and explained.[26] It is real now, useful now, helpful now. And by doing this they, in turn, 2) Preserve it for the future. They preserve the old paths for the future.[27] God's truth is not new, new-fangled, or faddish. God's truth is immutable. The same truth believed by the saints today should be the same truths believed by the saints of yesteryear. Why do Christians often *look back* to heroes of the faith in church history? What makes them heroes as such? They were lovers of the truth, lived by the truth, communicated that truth, and in all that were *resolved* to contend for it.

It is of utmost necessity that contending for the truth is accomplished by the church. "To the law and to

---

[26] "No man, when he hath lighted a candle, covereth it with a vessel, or putteth it under a bed; but setteth it on a candlestick, that they which enter in may see the light," (Luke 8:16).
[27] "Thus saith the LORD, Stand ye in the ways, and see, and ask for the old paths, where is the good way, and walk therein, and ye shall find rest for your souls," (Jer. 6:16).

the testimony: if they speak not according to this word, it is because there is no light in them," (Isa. 8:20). It is a distinguishing marker of a Christian either to be a contender or a pretender. Either a contender for the faith which they love, or a hypocrite by which they pretend to enter the kingdom of heaven; a form of godliness without its power. The saints of God are divinely commanded, by necessity, to be resolved in contending for the faith, in proclaiming it, and preserving it.

Are you not exceptionally happy, then, for the truths that have been published by God in his word and have been so preserved for you to read today? Without faithful saints who were contenders for the faith in bygone years, the saints today may have lost the truth, much less be able to contend for it. Imagine if Monica, Augustine's mother, did not pray. Imagine if she was not resolved to be a *contender* for the faith? What might church history look like? If Monica does not pray as she ought, (again, keep this thought in your mind, *who was the mother of Augustine*), Augustine might not have ever been converted. God used *her prayers* to aid her son's conversion by God's sovereign decree. Gottschalk, Aquinas, Wycliffe, Calvin, Luther and myriads more, all would never have read him. Where might *that* have gone? What if John Owen's wife treated him poorly and shunned the Scriptures, or walked disorderly, making his life quite the opposite of what it was? He might not have *ever* written anything. We would in turn have nothing of him to read today. And instead of pulling his

Mark 2: Resolved to Contend for the Faith

Death of Death in the Death of Christ off the shelf the first year of my college days, I might have never been introduced to the puritans. Who knows, then, where I might be today. Who knows, then, where *you* might be today had it not been for John Owen's wife, or the grandmother who prayed for you, the father that shared the truth with his children, the saint sharing a testimony to a newcomer to church ... there are a million billion scenarios in that way, and so many varied outcomes.

You are required to contend earnestly for the faith because that body of truth kindles your true affection for Christ. Christ, as King, has given express orders to all his subjects, to examine all spirits (1 John 4:1), all doctrines (2 John 1:9), at the judgment seat of the word of God, and to contend earnestly for the purity of his truth (1 Tim. 4:12), of his worship (John 4:24), of his ordinances, of his institutions, and the like. "Contend earnestly for the faith delivered," to *you*. Keeping the truth and holding to pure doctrine is not simply committed to ministers, or officers of Christ's church, but to the saints. To the whole church; it is a trust for which they are to be accountable. It should never, through their neglect, fall, as it were, into the gutters of the streets. Look around the country at but a glance, and you find whole denominations subverted from true worship, from fundamental Christian doctrines, for their warped acceptance of compromise, to satisfy the natural man's appetite, and to grow in numbers, by which they see as *success*. God says, be resolved, no matter what, *to contend for the faith*.

Your goal should be to have your hearts and minds set on the object of faith: God, Christ and "the love of God."[28] How were the saints, as Jude instructs, to be employed about contending for the faith? It was by keeping themselves *in the love of God*. Knowing the truth, standing on it, and acting in it, one is then *resolved to love it*. That was one of their primary goals as Christians, and it is to be one of yours as well.

What would people, who know you, say about you? If they were asked, "what do you think about so and so – what is their interest?" Examine yourself on that note. What do you earnestly love and contend for? Politics? Sports? Food? Candy? Movies? Family? Hobbies? What do you earnestly talk about? Consider it. Our Lord Jesus said, "For out of the abundance of the heart the mouth speaks," (Matt. 12:34). What do you love? What do you strive after? What are you resolved to do? What do you speak about often?

God commands us as the saints, to hold the truth in such a way that we contend earnestly for it. It should be in our hearts, and in our mouths overflowing onto each other while it is still called today (Heb. 3:13). In this as saints, we long for more of the Lord Jesus. Christ is the Word, and the Word is Christ, and to know Christ is to know the Word and to know the Word is to know Christ. People often say, "I want to know God more." "I

---

[28] 1 John 4:9; Jude 1:21.

want to have a deeper relationship to Jesus Christ." "How can I have that?" We say, read your bible, read good books about Scripture, go to church, come to fellowship, go to bible studies, have devotions each day, pray, and like. Take up God's prescribed rules for holiness, and his ordinances. Why do we say this? It is because you cannot know Jesus Christ unless you know the truth of God which is contained in the Bible. Even little children are indoctrinated to know this in the jingle – "Jesus loves me! This I know, *For the Bible tells me so.*" You must be resolved to *know your bible.*

God's Word has been given to you, entrusted to you, and is a love letter sent by Christ to you, to know more about him, to be drawn to his love, his work, his salvation. The more you know the Word and live it out, the closer you will be to the living Word, Christ Jesus, and grow as a contender of the faith entrusted to you. You will, as a supernatural outcome, be resolved in this. How can you possibly say that *you know* the Lord Jesus Christ, and not know his Word? You cannot fellowship or pray to a God you do not know. Much less, you cannot contend for the faith on behalf of Christ, which is a directive straight from Christ's throne room to your ear, into your heart and your conscience, without being resolved to do it. The truth of Scripture pushes us, thrusts us into a deeper relationship with Jesus Christ and to serve the Great King. If you recall, Jesus' exhortation to his disciples was not that they go out to make converts, but rather *disciples* (learners); and disciples are in a constant state of learning (Matthew 28:18-20). When you come into the sanctuary, into a Bible study, into fellowship with other Christians, what you should be seeking, what you should be after, is to have the Word of God ministered to you, and to minister the word in your life and speech.

This requires that you know the word of God so well that you can contend earnestly for the faith in all the ways that such *contending* might occur. If you are a saint, Jude tells you, soldier up to guard the truth of God, exemplify it, use it as it is the sword of the Spirit; be resolved in this. You are in a war. That is why time and time again the writers of Scripture, carried by the Holy Spirit, wrote down commands, statues and directives to you in military terms. (Helmets and swords and shields and such). This is what Jude has done with our word "contend." It is a word of resolute steadfastness. And not only that, it is to *contend earnestly;* encourage or beseech someone to some task, earnestly, with all your might. The war of Christianity is dangerous. It will put to the test your courage, and the strength of the grace which is in your heart. If we are lacking, we will be useless to the kingdom of God. There is a constant barrage of error and ruinous doctrine that comes against the church constantly to pull you away from Christ, who is the true Word. Christians must not just contend against error, but earnestly live it out the truth. Who goes into battle unprepared? How does the contender in boxing prepare to fight the heavyweight champion?

There are many months, maybe even years of training, to "contend" for that title. They do not suddenly just jump into the ring. That would be unwise. The Christian life is not the fictional movie *Rocky*. Paul took many years of preparation after his conversion to become a missionary (14 years). Preparation breeds contending, contending breeds publishing and it breeds preservation.

    Jude tells us that the church is liable to be infected with error if *you* are not contending earnestly for the truth. There may not be a more difficult age to live in than ours, where the truth is so watered down or discarded by so many churches and denominations and seminaries and elders and professing Christians. Such people think defenders of truth are divisive. But what is it that we contend for? Gold, silver, precious jewels; no, nothing so trite. As saints, we contend for the Word of God, we are resolved to do it in love and honor to the Christ. Contenders will always be unpopular because they are *narrow minded*. And that is because God, in his Word, *is narrow minded*. No matter how big or small the truth is in the Word, we are to contend for it. But, the greatest weight should be set on the fundamentals and essentials of religion, and the nature of God's worship. God, Christ, redemption, justification, sanctification, worship, sacraments, *etc.*, are to be resolved upon, and upheld in sound doctrine, in truth, in earnestly contending for it.

I want to take it one step further and give you some incredibly poignant Scriptures which show us the downfall of neglecting the truth of God. John 8:31-32, "Then Jesus said to those Jews who believed him, "If you abide in my word, you are my disciples indeed. And you shall know the truth, the truth shall make you free." *If,* is a very hard word in the Scriptures. This is a warning. Yes indeed! *If* you do not abide in his word, then, you are not a disciple. 1 Timothy 6:3, "If anyone does not adhere to the sound instruction of our Lord Jesus Christ and to godly teaching, he is conceited and understands nothing." This does not pertain to some things, but *nothing.* God said of his people in Hosea 4:6, "My people are destroyed for a lack of knowledge." Destroyed, ceased, cut off; and here God was speaking *to his church.* Galatians 1:8, "But If we or an angel from heaven, preach any other gospel to you than what we have preached to you, let him be eternally condemned. As we have said before, so now I say again, if anyone preaches any other gospel to you than what you have received, let him be eternally condemned." In self-reflection, this is one the scariest verses in the Scriptures, because of the outcome of those who think they have the truth and actually do not. God says if we change the truth, and believe or teach any other Gospel, we shall be *eternally condemned.* We must be resolved to love the truth once delivered to the saints, and guard it as something *precious.*

You must love the truth so much that you become *possessed of it.* Hold fast to the words of Jude, love the word of God so much that you are pressed to contend earnestly for God with all those around you encouraging them to the truth, and being encouraged that God uses you in such a manner. It requires that we believe the truth as once delivered to us *consistently* and with great resolution to continue in it. We must contend constantly for it. It can, very much so, become tiresome in our day with so many who are wayward. Your Christian duty rests on being a contender; not a Bible thumper, or a brow beater, or an antagonist. You ought never to be one who exasperates another; and never one who is in some *cage stage*. Overbearing, brow beating, antagonizing Christians are *useless* to the kingdom, and unwise in the way they deal with others. Championship contenders are not brute beasts swinging their arms like a flail in the ring. They are precisely trained contenders, who know the game so well they have *mastered* it. But, you must love the Gospel and the Lord of the Gospel enough to contend earnestly for it, and to be resolved in that duty.

You might say, "how might I particularly contend for the faith. How is this to be done by me personally?" Order your Christian life, all of your walk, exactly as you find their rule laid down in Scripture. Search out the truth. *Hold* to the truth no matter what. Contending is not simply in some basic profession, but the power of godliness and the love of God that will keep you steadfast to the end. Contend, if you will, simply against the powers of darkness who are out to destroy you, by standing steadfast in the faith in the power of the Holy Spirit for King Jesus. All sinful and careless living will expose you to temptations and not only so, but they will also loosen and unwind your souls from holding the truth closely. Love to Christ makes one "contend for the faith" and as Oliver Heywood said, "even by disputing and dying for Christ, if God calls him to it."[29]

Be resolved to contend for the faith entrusted to you, without wavering, that in the present day, and the time to come, that precious Gospel will be preserved until the coming of the Lord Jesus. Do this earnestly, and do it of necessity as becoming a saint of Christ, for the publishing and preservation of God's truth.

---

[29] Heywood, Oliver, *The Works of Oliver Heywood*, Volume 4, (Edinburgh: John Vint, 1827) 108.

MARK 3: Resolved to Reject All Earthlimindedness

Luke 17:32, "Remember Lot's wife."

This section of Scripture, Luke 17, speaks particularly about Christ's kingdom (verses 20-21). Christ was replying to the Pharisees who had asked him a question about the *coming* of the kingdom. The particular question at hand really surrounded the Gospel. It surrounded the fulfillment of God's promises in the good tidings of the Scriptures, *i.e.* the kingdom of God breaking into the world by the Messiah. It surrounds, Luke 17:20, "when the kingdom of God would come…" When Jesus answers them, there are two lines of thought that are related here which deal with, 1) His coming in light of the destruction of Jerusalem, and 2) His coming at the end of the world. It is a discussion of the basic theme: the kingship of Christ or kingdom of God.[30] In order to understand what follows it should be understood that in the Greek the word for *kingdom* sometimes means kingship (rule, reign, sovereignty), as well as kingdom itself. Unless this fact is kept in mind, one will experience some difficulty in understanding verses 20-21.[31]

---

[30] See my work, *God Reigns as King* for a full discussion of this topic.
[31] See my sermons at Grace Chapel on the "kingdom" for a full teaching of this idea.

Asked by the Pharisees when the kingdom of God would come, Jesus replied by saying, the kingdom of God does not come with outward display, "nor will people say, Look, here it is! or there it is! for," *note well,* "the kingdom of God is within you." The Pharisees and their many followers were looking forward to the arrival of an outward, earthly, visible kingdom, one in which the Jews would occupy a very prominent place. They were hardly able to wait for its arrival. They certainly *knew* about the kingdom, and even in the preaching of John the Baptist and Jesus, the two Elijah and Elisha's of God's fulfillment, preached with desiring an immediate response to something the Jews of the day would have understood. John said, "Repent ye: for the kingdom of heaven is at hand," (Matt. 3:2). Jesus equally preached, "Repent: for the kingdom of heaven is at hand," (Matt. 4:17). And the Apostles were sent out to preach in the same way, "And as ye go, preach, saying, The kingdom of heaven is at hand," (Matt. 10:7). Yet, Jews were misinformed about their *interpretation* of the kingdom which was to come. Jesus declares that the kingdom, or here preferably *kingship or reign or rule of God*, is spiritual in its essence. It is within, or, if one prefers, *inside a believing convert.* Wherever God is truly recognized and honored as King, there one finds his kingdom or kingship.

In Luke 17:22-25, he then spoke to his disciples, "Then He said to the disciples, "The days will come when you will desire to see one of the days of the Son of

Man, and you will not see it. "And they will say to you, `Look here!' or `Look there!' Do not go after them or follow them. "For as the lightning that flashes out of one part under heaven shines to the other part under heaven, so also the Son of Man will be in His day," (Luke 17:22-24). The Pharisees are now not the center of attention, and Jesus directs his speech to the disciples. These words are spoken to Christ's followers, both at that time, and subsequently to all resolved disciples down through the ages. Note the following: the phrase "the days of the Son" signifies "the Messianic era" at the close of the world's history.[32] Some thought that this kingdom was to come immanently, right now, and in considering this, there was an eager expectation of excitement but without knowledge. The Bridegroom tarries,[33] the Nobleman goes to a far country and tarries,[34] the Lord even says, "If I will that he tarry till I come, what is that to thee?" (John 21:22). Even wicked servants know that the Lord could come back at any time, but that he is currently delayed though there is work to be done now.[35] However, when the coming of the Lord occurs, it will be worldwide, and there will be no mistaking it.

---

[32] See my work, *Seeing Christ Clearly* for a full consideration of the coming of the Son of Man in his message and mission.

[33] "...while the bridegroom tarried," (Matt. 25:5).

[34] "A certain nobleman went into a far country to receive for himself a kingdom, and to return. And he called his ten servants, and delivered them ten pounds, and said unto them, *Occupy till I come*," (Luke 19:12-13).

[35] "My lord delayeth his coming," (Matt. 24:48).

When the end happens, *no one* will miss it.[36] It is coming, and it could arrive at any time. But no one knows when that will be, so watch, pray and be prepared.

Jesus says that before he comes, suffering comes first. The words, "and must be rejected by this generation," show that Jesus was pointing to the cross. "But first He must suffer many things and be rejected by this generation," (Luke 17:25). Having spoken about his second coming and about his suffering that is to occur much earlier, Jesus now pictures how people will be living during the days just before his final return at the end of the ages.

Consider, verses 26-27, "And just as it was in the days of Noah..." *etc.* The very suddenness of his coming points to the necessity of guarding against being unprepared and being careless. "And as it was in the days of Noah, so it will be also in the days of the Son of Man: They ate, they drank, they married wives, they were given in marriage, until the day that Noah entered the ark, and the flood came and destroyed them all," (Luke 17:26-27). They were unconcerned, far from being resolved to follow the great King. They continued to live "as always," eating and drinking, marrying and giving in marriage. The men of Noah's day failed to realize their perilous situation until it was too late. Though Noah

---

[36] "Behold, he cometh with clouds; and every eye shall see him, and they also which pierced him," (Rev. 1:7).

Mark 3: Resolved to Reject All Earthlimindedness

preached as a preacher of righteousness, people did not listen. Sadly, it is no different today.

Suddenly, for those in Noah's day, the cataclysm occurred, where the word used in the original "came" was indeed a "washing down," which is the basic meaning of the word. In other words, the flood destroyed them all, and no one saw it coming except Noah.

And, verses 28-30, "So also it was in the days of Lot..." *etc.* "Likewise as it was also in the days of Lot: They ate, they drank, they bought, they sold, they planted, they built; "but on the day that Lot went out of Sodom it rained fire and brimstone from heaven and destroyed them all. "Even so will it be in the day when the Son of Man is revealed," (Luke 17:28-30). The people of Lot's day were also engaged in the ordinary affairs of life: eating and drinking, buying and selling, planting and building. But they were utterly self-centered. Lot lived among them, as a righteous man who was distressed by their *filthy lives* (2 Peter 2:7-8). His soul was vexed daily while being among such vile people.

As the historical narrative describes, Lot left Sodom by God's command. Jesus is attesting to both Noah and Lot's personal realities and occurrences in being resolved. With Noah, it was destruction by water. With Lot, it was the destruction of Sodom and Gomorrah by fire. In Sodom, fire and sulfur rained down from heaven and destroyed them all, including outlying towns. Why did Christ select Noah and Lot as examples of men who took heed, *were resolved*, against those who did not? Both Noah and Lot were not as virtuous as one would like. Noah is known not only for building an ark, but then getting drunk and exposing himself. Lot lived in *Sodom*. What was he thinking? The examples surround belief and resolution; that both *heeded* God's warning. Noah built an ark, and Lot left Sodom. Water drowned the world in the first, and fire destroyed the cities in the second. So, Jesus says, it will be also on the day "the Son of Man" at his coming is revealed in all his glory.

Verse 31. On that day... *etc.* "In that day, he who is on the housetop, and his goods are in the house, let him not come down to take them away. And likewise the one who is in the field, let him not turn back," (Luke 17:31). In Matthew 24:17-18 and its parallel Mark 13:15-16, this warning is applied to the days just previous to Jerusalem's fall (A.D. 70). The meaning of these passages is that the man who is on the flat roof of his house—from which by means of an outside ladder he can descend in order as quickly as possible to flee to the hills—must not, after descending, enter his house in order to rescue any of his goods. Similarly, the laborer, dressed only in his tunic and in this way working in the field, must not before his flight to the hills go back into his house to get his coat. Both of these men should flee at once, without trying to rescue any possessions, whether a coat or anything else. In connection with the present passage any thought of fleeing is, of course, out of the question.

Mark 3: Resolved to Reject All Earthlimindedness

To this admonition Jesus adds a short illustrative proverb. Yes, *preachers like illustrations.* However, to ride the soap box for a moment, poorly used illustrations are what make up most of contemporary preaching today. They merely fill up sermons and get the congregation off to lunch quickly. Rightly used illustrations become, what the divines called, proverbs. These are short pithy sayings which sum up the idea of what is being taught. The illustration Christ uses shows the tragic result of looking back with yearning to possessions that have been left behind, desiring to hold onto that which is familiar. And in this illustration, he concluded by telling them to remember the plight of Lot's wife looking back to earthly things in Sodom.

    The doctrine to consider here is verse 32, "Remember Lot's wife!" This is Christ's warning to those whose hearts are enflamed for the world. There is an element of turning back in earthlimindedness. Lot's wife was infected with that which caused her to turn back; she had a worldly heart. If the heart is attached to the world, there is no escaping the consequences of sin and misery no matter how far one runs away from physical place itself.

    It is not that the disciples listening should consider her sad estate being turned simply into a pillar of salt. But, that in her scale of values, she placed earth above heaven, material things above spiritual. She was earthliminded. She was *not* resolved to heed God's word, or to follow God's directions, or even to follow her godly husband. She longed for earthly things instead.

What Jesus holds before his followers, then, is that they should be so prepared for his return that in their thoughts, words, and deeds, they always assign the pre-eminence to him, doing everything out of love for him, and in this way for God as servants of the Great King. They are *resolved* in this, without wavering, without turning back to the world.

It is especially profound in Christ's simple phrase which begins with *remember.* There are only three classifications in Scripture of Christ's use of the word to remember. "Remember" what he teaches – he teaches his word and people are to remember his word. "Remember the word that I said unto you," (John 15:20). Remember his broken body and shed blood in the Lord's Supper. "This is my body which is given for you: this do in remembrance of me," (Luke 22:19). And, "Remember Lot's wife" in light of his *coming.* Why? Verse 33, "Whoever tries to keep his life shall lose it, but whoever loses (his life) shall preserve it." In the present context those who are represented as trying to hang on to their life, and losing it, are the earth-bound people of Noah's day and of Lot's day, including the poignant illustration of Lot's wife, and all those similarly minded.

Consider her sin, and, consider her punishment. Her sin was a secret heart sin that *only she and God knew.* Her punishment fit the sin, and God acted speedily to render justice on her.[37] These are indeed losers of the kingdom which will become apparent especially on the day of Christ's return. On that day, the preservation and victory of the people who have shown the opposite attitude, that of self-denial and self-sacrifice, out of love for their Savior with a hearty resolve, will become publicly manifest. Wherever there are those who are spiritually dead, there the final judgment will overtake them.

Who was this woman? Who was Lot's wife? Genesis 19:1-26 gives the account. She was the wife of a man with many faults, yet God considered Lot righteous. She was united to him by matrimony. She had lived among Abraham, and the working of God in Abraham's life. She shared in all the privileges of the separated people, and yet she perished. She was dear to Lot, who had been dear to father Abraham, the father of the faithful, and still she perished in her sin. Think about it – she followed her husband out of the city, she was actually out of Sodom, she was almost in Zoar, the refuge city, and yet she perished. "Almost saved, but not quite." Like Agrippa, "...almost a Christian," (Acts 26:28). But almost a Christian is *not* a Christian. An inch away from hell is as much as an infinite measure from heaven.

Lot's wife *fled* Sodom. She went with her husband and her daughters. She seemed to be righteous,

---

[37] This is reminiscent of God's speedy judgment on Nadab and Abihu for their false (earthlyminded) worship with strange fire in Leviticus 10.

and seemed to be of God's people. Some in Sodom may have seemed to carry a pleasant face, and make an outward show of goodness, but what about their inward disposition? If one could look into their heart, such people are altogether filthy and abominable. Make note, she *lingered behind Lot.* Moses tells us, "Lot's wife looked back from *behind him.*" She was a slacker, drawn away with the enticements of the earthly kingdom. Staying as close to it as she could for as long as she could.

Sadly, Lot's wife looked back to Sodom. She didn't realize Sodom had nothing, spiritually speaking, to offer. Not realizing this was a sign of her lost condition. All the enjoyments of Sodom would perish, and they will all be burned up. Archeologically, Sodom's excavation demonstrates that the city was so pummeled, that it laid under two feet of ash, where no structure was left standing and all that remain were fragments of the foundations of the city. Archeologists say that the impact of the fire from the heavens would have been like hundreds of atomic bombs all exploding at one time. Was this worth looking back to? No. It is not worth looking back on things that are perishing and consuming in the flames, as it is with all the enjoyments of sin. They are all appointed to the spiritual fire. "No man, having put his hand to the plough, and looking back, is fit for the kingdom of God," (Luke 9:62).

Lot's wife remembered the joy in those things that she left in Sodom. Sodom was a place of great abundance for her. Remember why Lot chose that region? It was because the soil around Sodom was exceedingly fruitful. It is said to be as the garden of God, (Gen. 13:10). And, fullness of bread was one of the sins of the place, (Ezek. 16:49), as was idleness, which is the devil's workshop.

Lot's wife sinned against the express directive of God. In disobeying such a command, she was filled with the world, and with unbelief. "If you look back, you will die," the angel warned them. "If you go forward, you will live." The Israelites, later, would not learn from her. After being delivered from Egyptian bondage, they wanted to *go back to Egypt* because of the difficulty of their trials. Did Moses have such ideas in mind as he penned, by the direction of the Holy Spirit, not only the description of "the pillar of salt," but the words that the Israelites would murmur about such things? Such was the case of Demas, according to Paul, who loved the world and went back to it. "For Demas hath forsaken me, having loved this present world," (2 Tim. 4:10).

Lot's wife loved Sodom. She loved earthly things more than godly things. She was warned by messengers sent from God to make haste to leave Sodom, and not even to look behind her at it. There is nothing wrong with the things of life so long as they are used for the glory of God, and not for selfish reasons. When the soul becomes entirely wrapped up in them, so that matters such as these become ends in themselves, and spiritual tasks are neglected, they are no longer a blessing but have become a curse. They have become evidences of gross materialism, false security, and often cold selfishness.

Looking back may seem like a *small* thing, but the reader of that narrative can be sure, by its punishment, that it was a great sin ... exceedingly sinful and detestable to God. Lot's wife disobeyed a precise command, and mimicked the same kind of rebellion as Adam did in the garden. *Unbelief* was at its core. Maybe she questioned whether Sodom would be destroyed, and thought she *might* still have been safe in it. She chose her will over God's will. She looked back on her neighbors whom she had left behind with more concern than was fitting. Now that their day of grace was over, and divine justice was glorifying itself in their ruin, she also partook of that. She loved her house and goods in Sodom, and was loath to leave them. Christ demonstrates this to be her sin, for she regarded her "stuff" too much. Her "looking back" has in it an evidence of her *inclination* to go back; a bosom sin. Therefore, Christ uses it as a general warning against apostasy from the Christian profession. Christians are to renounce the world, the flesh and the devil, and have their faces set toward heaven, whose builder and maker are God. They are now in the plain of Zoar, and they are supposed to be resolved to get there without lagging behind. They are now in their probation. It is at their peril if they return to the interests they profess by their leaving to have abandoned. Drawing back is an exercise towards perdition, and looking back is a *desire* of such things.

Such a judgment against Lot's wife was quite, 1) sudden, and, 2) extraordinary. Consider that it was 1) *sudden*. Sometimes God is very terrible out of his holy places. In the midst of saving the family from destruction, she did not regard God's terrible judgment. So, God was immediate in his judgment. It was also, 2) extraordinary. There is no other person turned into a pillar of salt other than Lot's wife anywhere in Scripture. She has no name. It is not given. But she is *remembered*. What is enough is to remember that she was turned into a pillar of salt. It housed an element of eternal shame on this sin being recorded for all time in Scripture, not to mention, that for whatever time her public statue stood in the plain of Zoar, it was a memorial for all who came upon it. Jesus says it is a memorial for all his disciples to *remember her*.

The city of Sodom was exceedingly wicked. What did Jesus think of Sodomites? Sodom is representative of a city full of filthiness and abominations. Jonathan Edwards described it this way, "It is full of those impurities that ought to be had in the utmost abhorrence and detestation by all. The inhabitants of it are a polluted company. They are all under the power and dominion of hateful lusts. All their faculties and affections are polluted with those vile dispositions that are unworthy of the human nature, that greatly debase it, that are exceedingly hateful to God, and that dreadfully incense his anger. Every kind of spiritual abomination abounds in it. There is nothing so hateful and abominable but that there it is to be found, and there it abounds."[38] Sodom and Gomorrah were cities filled with devils and all manner of unclean spirits. Who would be so foolish as to have their hearts trapped by such a city? Who would not flee from such a city with haste?

Sodom and her inhabitants were appointed to destruction. God had heard the cry of their wickedness which was exceedingly great. He will not allow such a city to stand. God is holy, and his nature is infinitely opposed to everything Lot's wife desired about the city. They were appointed to destruction without pity. How could it be that Lot's wife wanted to go back? Literally, Sodom suffered the vengeance of eternal fire. Jude 1:7, "Even as Sodom and Gomorrah, and the cities about them, in like manner, giving themselves over to fornication, and going after strange flesh, are set forth for an example, suffering the vengeance of eternal fire." The destruction that Sodom and Gomorrah suffered was a picture of eternal destruction. All that is left in that place is ash, sulfur and salt. It was fitting that she too be turned into a pillar of salt...down to her very core. No one who was truly a citizen of Sodom would escape. All would be reduced to salt; and this would have included, in retrospect, Lot's wife. Jude says that they were set forth *as an example*, a type or representation of the

---

[38] Edwards, Jonathan, *Sermons and Discourses, 1734–1738*, ed. M. X. Lesser and Harry S. Stout, vol. 19, The Works of Jonathan Edwards (New Haven; London: Yale University Press, 2001), 324.

eternal fire in which all the ungodly are to be consumed (Jude 1:7). Why would Lot's wife *so desire* to be included in the company of those who resemble the eternal damnation and swift destruction of God upon wickedness?

The application of this whole idea is rather simplistic, but very important. "Remember Lot's wife." Christ *commanded* his disciples to *remember* her. That includes us. It is profitable for us to meditate and ponder this passage, be resolved to never be like her or mimic her.

Lot's wife is remembered for her worldly lusts, for loving the world more than she loved God; for her unbelief; for an everlasting monument of shame. This is inscribed, as it were, with a pen of iron in the Scriptures. It is *so monumental* that our Lord uses it as an illustration to sum up his teaching of his final coming and judgment. Where will *your* eyes be? No, better yet, *where is your heart?* Was it really a matter of sight for her? Was it really simply a *look* that turned her into salt? No, it was a sinful disposition that caused her to look back, in opposition to holding onto holiness, being unresolved to dismiss all her earthlimindedness. She did not hold steadfastly to God's spiritual goodness, and the promise of blessing, and desired the sins of Sodom over the blessing of deliverance.

The world of humanity falls into two families. Those who live in the city of God and those who live in the city of man; those of the line of the woman, and those of the line of the serpent. Being converted, and in the company of Zion and the righteous, at no time will Christ allow us to look back to that which we fled from without recourse. Every one of you who have been saved by the Son of Man, have been delivered from a fate even worse than the physical city of Sodom. As much as Christ encourages and cultivates your love, joy, grace, mercy and all the other choice blessings that are found only in him and through him, he still warns...who? *His disciples.* So, "Remember Lot's wife." Be resolved to never look back to the remembrance of the enjoyments which you have had in Sodom, and never cultivate any of the same enjoyments now that you had then in the same manner.

Remember Lot's wife. She looked back and was sad that she was leaving a life of ease and comfort in the carnal city. You must be forever willing to leave all the ease, and pleasure, and profit of sin, to forsake all for Christ. The only way that salvation works for the Christian's good is to press forward with all their might, and still to look and press forward, never to stand still or slow-down in their pace, *to always be resolved* to serve King Jesus. When Lot's wife stopped in her flight and stood still in order that she might look, her punishment was, that there she was to stand forever; she never got any further; she never got beyond that place; unable to take a single step further. But there she stood as a pillar of salt, a memorial, a permanent pillar and monument of wrath, for her folly and wickedness. So, it will be with those who fall into apostasy, though they may live what looks to be a Christian walk for a long time. What will happen? When they seem to be Christians, they instead look back. They may have even taken some pains for their "salvation," and yet, in looking back, in taking their hand off the plow, they lose everything, not being fit for the Kingdom of God.

What happens to professing Christian backsliders who look back? Such people quench the Spirit of God. They lose their convictions and become discouraged. They begin to harden their hearts towards the means of grace. They begin to strengthen and establish the interest of bosom-sins in their hearts. They give way to Satan. Their souls *harden* like a pillar of salt, like Lot's wife, one which has lost all its savor. They provoke God willingly in practical atheism where they *act like* atheists.

When you begin down the road of apostasy, there is a *great danger;* it cannot be understated. Hebrews 10:26-27 says, "For if we sin willfully after we have received the knowledge of the truth, there no longer remains a sacrifice for sins, but a certain fearful expectation of judgment, and fiery indignation which will devour the adversaries." The devil doesn't come to you with a pitchfork and red pajamas. He comes as an angel of light (just as he did with Adam and Eve in the garden), to draw you slowly away, so that though you might not jump off the cliff at the beginning, his intention is to get you off the cliff ultimately. A little closer, a little closer, a little wedge of gold like Achan, a little of the world to gain back again like Demas, a little *peek* like Lot's wife. *What would it hurt?* The devil's intention all along is to rustle up sin in you that it might draw you back and entice you to commit that evil against God. And the devil is quite patient. He will let Lot's wife progress *right up* to the plain of Zoar, almost to the city, and then turn for a short glimpse.

Remember Christ's words about remembering Lot's wife. Apostacy usually comes on people that have for some time been under any considerable convictions, and afterwards *lose* them. These are people with no godly resolve. Matthew 13:22, "Now he who received seed among the thorns is he who hears the word, and the cares of this world and the deceitfulness of riches choke the word, and he becomes unfruitful."

Considering her outcome should press us to great care and great diligence in our walk before God. Looking back to sin is a great cause of grief and misery. *It's just a look?* Looks tells us what our hearts are like. It is the opposite of separating one's self to Christ in holy living. Looks are the first outward expressions of inward dispositions.

Don't simply *remember* Lot's *wife*, but remember *why Christ commanded us to remember her*. It is in respect to his final coming, to live accordingly in light of what Lot's wife did. His warning to us discriminates between us acting like Lot, or acting like his wife. We are to be resolved to live life in a manner which is *holy;*

for *without holiness no one will see the Lord.* It is a resolute life lived in the eager expectation of his tarried return.

Lot's wife disobeyed God's command and failed to heed his warning; could God have been any clearer? "Escape for your life! Do not look behind you, and do not stay anywhere in the valley; escape to the mountains, lest you be swept away," (Gen. 19:17). Is God unjust to repay disobedience with a previously announced penalty? Evidently Jesus did not think so, for he admonished his hearers, "Remember Lot's wife" (Luke 17:32).

This account teaches us to treat holiness as something *precious*. If you want to be a Christian you must never change your purpose: you must not look for another way or another Gospel, or another path, or an easier way. There is yet one and only one way to the city of refuge, and it requires you not to ever look back. If you attempt to enter heaven by some other way than the way of Jesus Christ, you are perishing and are like Lot's wife. If the Christian life becomes too tedious, and too hard, and too demanding, and you consider, "Should I go back?" *Remember Lot's wife.*

But so far as Lot's wife is concerned, this example is instructive for us rather than simply a condemnation of the woman. She was overcome by spiritual and human weakness and, contrary to the angels' command, looked back toward the awful sounds she heard about that which she loved. The allurements of the world should never draw us aside from the meditation of the heavenly life. Salvation in Christ is not simply about how you start, but it is *especially* how you end up; have you run to win the prize so that you take your foot and run it over and passed the finish line? This takes biblical *resolve*. Lot's wife was literally at the gate, and did not make it in. She perished in the very act of sin because her heart was being tugged by the whispers of the world. She was lagging behind in the back, and she had no qualms about stealing, like Achan, a little of *something*, and for her it was a final glance at her home, her house, her friends, her neighborhood, the longing of her heart. What would a *little look* do? Her husband did not see her turn and steal a glance at Sodom, because he did not look back, ... but God saw her. God knows the depths of every heart. Christ's teaching concerns the *hearts* of his disciples. It is about practical atheism, or, a real biblical resolution. Doing what we want, rather than what God says, no matter how big or small it might be is the question in the scales and balance of Christ's words here. A preacher by the name of Theophilus Gale gave a sermon in which the title was, "How the Love of the World is Inconsistent with the Love of God." In other words, these two things are diametrically opposed. They are contrary to one another. How can one love the world, and love Christ? How can you serve two masters? Consider this in the words of Augustine, "Remember

Lot's wife (Luke 17:32), think on that pillar of salt, that it may season you."[39]

---

[39] Augustine, "Reply to Faustus the Manichæan," in *St. Augustine: The Writings against the Manichaeans and against the Donatists*, ed. Philip Schaff, trans. Richard Stothert, vol. 4, <u>A Select Library of the Nicene and Post-Nicene Fathers of the Christian Church, First Series,</u> (Buffalo, NY: Christian Literature Company, 1887), 288.

MARK 4: Resolved to Righteously Use the Means of Grace

"The word that came to Jeremiah from the LORD, saying, Stand in the gate of the LORD'S house, and proclaim there this word, and say, Hear the word of the LORD, all ye of Judah, that enter in at these gates to worship the LORD. Thus saith the LORD of hosts, the God of Israel, Amend your ways and your doings, and I will cause you to dwell in this place. Trust ye not in lying words, saying, The temple of the LORD, The temple of the LORD, The temple of the LORD, are these. For if ye thoroughly amend your ways and your doings; if ye thoroughly execute judgment between a man and his neighbor; If ye oppress not the stranger, the fatherless, and the widow, and shed not innocent blood in this place, neither walk after other gods to your hurt: Then will I cause you to dwell in this place, in the land that I gave to your fathers, for ever and ever. Behold, ye trust in lying words, that cannot profit," (Jer. 7:1-8).

In Pre-exilic Judah, before the exile of the church, king Nebopolassar dies mysteriously in God's providence around 604 B.C. The king of Babylon is now Nebuchadnezzar who takes his place as God's "signet ring." He will be the stamp of God's power. There is much about Nebuchadnezzar to study, such as the rise, the fall and restoration of this wayward king brought *savingly* to God.[40] The king of Judah is Jehoiachin, "Jehoiachin was eighteen years old when he became king, and he reigned in Jerusalem three months. His mother's name was Nehushta the daughter of Elnathan of Jerusalem. And he did evil in the sight of the LORD, according to all that his father had done," (2 King 24:8-9). Jehoiachin and Mattaniah (later Zedekiah) were most likely present at the temple on, "the important days of worship." "At the turn of the year King Nebuchadnezzar summoned him and took him to Babylon, with the costly articles from the house of the LORD, and made Zedekiah, Jehoiakim's brother, king over Judah and Jerusalem," (2 Chron. 36:10).

God promises coming judgment at this time, through Jeremiah, his weeping prophet. In previous chapters we find that Judah is in for it worse than her sister Israel who was conquered in 606 B.C. Jeremiah even delivers this warning to Judah using Israel as the example. "Is Israel a servant? Is he a homeborn slave? Why is he plundered? The young lions roared at him, and growled; they made his land waste; his cities are burned, without inhabitant," (Jer. 2:14-15). The *riff-raff* rise up here, where the response of false prophets contradict God's message in Jeremiah 2:8. They have sacrificed to Baal mustering what help "they could." The

---

[40] For an excellent treatment of this, consider reading *The Pride, Fall and Restitution of King Nebuchadnezzar*, by Henry Smith (1550–1591).

text reads, "The priests did not say, "Where is the LORD?" And those who handle the law did not know Me; The rulers also transgressed against Me; The prophets prophesied by Baal, And walked after things that do not profit," (Jer. 2:8). In Jeremiah 5:13 they are described as "blow hards" and "wind bags," feeding the people lies in contrast to what God is doing. Through Jeremiah, God desires to feed his people, sending, in Jeremiah 3:15, "feeders who will feed you..." or, pastors who will be under-shepherds. In contrast, these false prophets are not heralds of truth. "And the prophets become wind, For the word is not in them," (Jer. 5:13). This is the brief backdrop to the verses for this chapter.

Jeremiah's exhortation to be considered is in 7:1-8. God speaks to Jeremiah (chapters 1-6), now Jeremiah speaks to the people (chapters 7 and following). He says, "Stand in the gate of the Lord's house..." Literally "take your stand, or be planted there." False prophets have no problem voicing their opinion. Most likely, this occurred at the time of a feast, where all would be present. What would he do? He was commissioned to "...proclaim there the word." The use of the word "proclaim" is the Hebrew meaning "be read aloud, and to summon." It can even extrapolate to "call them out on their sin." He does this *through* God's word. This "word" is a "law case" or "legal matter" God has against his people. In fact, God had an *air tight case* against them and Jeremiah was to proclaim it to them. This was as about a stressful situation for Jeremiah as could be, since

Jeremiah was in the midst of the temple as a priest, and he was, for all intents and purposes, *on his own*, humanly speaking. And yet, he was *resolved* to follow God's lead.

He addressed those "...that enter into these gates to worship the Lord." Were the people there to do what the Lord commanded? They were there to *worship*. It is even what the text says. This is the very reason why you have a temple and sacrificial system – to come and worship the Lord! The phrase "worship the Lord" is common throughout the Scriptures; it is not very special in any word-choice regard. But there *is* a problem. Jeremiah 6:20 says, "your burnt offerings are not acceptable, nor your sacrifices sweet unto me." Casual worship, *the casual use* of the means of grace, is never acceptable no matter how much the people might think they are doing what is right.[41]

Jeremiah instructs them, "Amend your ways and your doings..." meaning to *do good to, deal well with; to do well,* and to *do right*. Resolve yourselves to amend your ways, "to do right, or righteously," with God. Religious syncretism (mixing false worship with true worship) had crippled them. They had sacrificed to false gods, and the rulers of the nation, (king, priests and prophets), had led them astray. They mixed their worship with heathenish worship. This God detests. What does God wish the covenant people of Judah to

---

[41] The church at large should take a note on that point in their own worship today.

know? He wants them to reform! Get to the business of being *covenant people*. Get to the business of *reformation*.

If they do, God says, "...I will cause you to dwell in this place." A promise of God based on repentance is given. In Scripture, this kind of statement is called *a declaration*. God prescribes an *if...then* scenario to them. What will happen? What will they do? God calls them to act, to repent, to change their mind. What were their minds enraptured by?

"Do not trust in these lying words," (Jer. 7:4) The specifics of repentance were missed. They needed to see this: *do not do what you have been doing*. Literally do not "place confidence in..." these lying words. Even more to the point, for this passage, "do not live carelessly," before the means of grace. They have every opportunity to live well before God. Everything they needed for true spiritual worship and drawing near to the Savior, God provided. They could, if they simply listened to his word, live well.

What are these lying words? The lying words are, "...saying the Temple of the Lord, the Temple of the Lord, the Temple of the Lord...these." The temple is temporary, a tool used to foreshadow the coming of God's Messiah who would fulfill all the types and shadows to do away with temples and sacrifices and ceremonies and such. They are not a means to be ultimately trusted in as they are *in themselves*. They have no moral goodness in them apart from the work of

Mark 4: Resolved to Righteously Use the Means of Grace

King Jesus the Messiah. After the Lord Jesus Christ comes and fulfills the Scriptures, there is no more use for the temple by anyone, for any purpose, at any time, ever in the future history of the church. "It is finished," Jesus said. The veil is torn upon his death on the cross, and God later destroys this temple where one stone is not left upon another in the establishment of fulfilled Christian truth. At this time, though, the shadow of the temple and all its ceremonies existed as a symbolic place of God's presence. The translation is better suited to say "these" not "are these." As if one would stretch out their hands to symbolically embrace all "this" that God has given the people. "Look at what he has given. Look at the place of atonement. Look at the place of prayer. Look where the word is read. Look where instruction from the priests takes place. Look where the blood is spilt and sprinkled. Look where God's presence resides above the mercy seat." Look at ... *these!* Why three times is this repeated though? There are two reasons: the repetition is placed as an interpretive help. It is a literary device of exclamation! Other places where this occurs are positive in scope such as Isaiah 6 (holy, holy, holy) and through the Gospels as Jesus will say "Truly, truly." Also, this triple use of the "temple of the Lord" refers to the three tiers of the temple; the court, the holy place and holy of holies. These three places represent where the people come (court). Where the priests work (holy place). Where the sacrifice is sprinkled on the ark of the covenant in God's presence (holy of holies). In the mouth of Jeremiah God gives a poetic use of the means of grace hypocritically exploited by these apostatizing people. They trusted in their hypocrisy because they merely *had* the means of grace. But *merely having them* is not a recipe for a good spiritual use of them.

Judah lived *carelessly* before the means of grace. They believed that since God was symbolically in their midst in the temple, they were safe, because they thought that they were *the* chosen people, *God's* holy nation. God had chosen them over the Philistines, over the Amorites, over the Jebusites, *etc.* "We have the forgiveness of sins!" "We have Yom Kippur!" Little do they know that not so far into the future, God sends his Messiah to fulfill and eradicate such things from the earth, has the temple pillaged, then has the temple destroyed. He gave them two visual warnings of the reality of their transgressions at two different times over a period of hundreds of years in such judgment as a precursor to the Messiah. This was to point to the coming of Christ, and their failure to use the means of God's grace in a righteous manner. They misused the means of grace at this time, which was using the temple in the wrong way. The temple was their only hope of atonement; but they abused it, and abused God's mercy.

They used the temple as they saw fit, instead of the only means rightly employed through the resolved conviction of God's truth. It was more of a *heritage* instead of the saving means of grace. It was a desire to use it their own way, rather than God's way. They were *blatant idolaters* in this. They exchanged the truth of God for a lie and denied their only sovereign and Lord. The wrath of God which comes after the bestowal of the means of grace, and the longsuffering of God's patience without having biblical fruit to show for, is often intensely severe against the ungodly who live carelessly before it. Francis Roberts said, "The greater God's patience, and means of grace on earth, if fruitless, the greater will be the damnation and torments of the wicked in hell."[42] Ultimately, when we look just a bit further into their history, when the Messiah came, they lost everything and God severely judged them.

The doctrine to consider here as it relates to Christian resolve is this: it is a soul-destroying sin to live carelessly before God's ordained means of grace. This sin applies equally to all kinds of people. Sin will throw the Christian off course, and it will bar the path for the sinner to find the narrow road. It reverses and impairs a resolute spirit.

How might one define "careless living?" To "live" is a state of being. To live "carelessly" could be defined as a reckless disposition of apathy. Sometimes such people *do not even care about caring*. The priests, the king and the people did not care about caring, or anything of spiritual worth in this matter. They were happy enough with their traditions.

---

[42] Roberts, Francis, *Mysterium & Medulla Bibliorum*, (London: R.W. for George Calvert, 1657), 254.

How might one define "God-ordained?" God defines the proper means in which sinners are to approach him. God sets them down, writes them down, inscribes them in his word as if with a pen or iron and expects them to be followed by his covenant people. He does this for all his means of grace. He ordains such things for the good of his people.

How might one define "means of grace?" The means of grace are the only methods and manners by which men are saved or sanctified in Jesus Christ, in the Old Testament or New Testament. That which points to or directly communicates the way of salvation that God has given in Jesus Christ is the means God uses to sanctify people. These are means which are gracious, given by God, but gain saving or sanctifying grace for the believer. The means of grace are ordinances *of God;* there are no others. There was no *temple number two* in another city (as much as the Samaritans would have liked it to be so with their version of worship at their temple). Keeping it simple, a Bible bought in Wal-Mart is a means of grace. One might say, "you have made a leap from the temple, to that which God uses through Christ the Messiah in the word of God. Aren't these things very different?" Not at all. These things are not different because the substance of what makes them "the means of grace" is Jesus Christ, regardless of what age the church is in, or what testament we look to. The history of the early church or the *older church* makes no difference in its Gospel substance. Regardless of what

Mark 4: Resolved to Righteously Use the Means of Grace

testament we look to, God's doctrine is always the same. Grace is *only* found in Jesus Christ, and Christians pray that God would indeed bestow and bless all the means of grace to them.[43]

What are the means of grace? The means of grace are God-ordained instruments of special grace, used in a specific context, where grace offered removes sin and renews the sinner in conformity with the image of God through Jesus Christ in the power of the Spirit. At the time, these means revolved around the ceremonial sacrificial system attached to the Moral Law. These ceremonies are shadows of what Christ would accomplish in his fulfillment of their types. His work made those means effective for those people at that time who were truly converted. They believed, by faith, the shadows pointed to God's Messiah who would fulfill all things God had decreed and ordained for salvation. They are the means by which the Holy Spirit operates. In our passage, emphasis is given to the "word", and the spiritual power of the Word is dependent only on the operation of the Holy Spirit in the mouth of God's ordained minister.

The means of grace are the official instruments that God has given his church. What are those official

---

[43] Question 195 of the *Westminster Larger Catechism*. Further, that there would be no "unfruitfulness under the means of grace," (*The Directory of Public Worship*). The Directory also states that in regards to the sacrament of baptism, "the sufferings and merits of the Lord Jesus Christ the Son of God," are the spiritual means by which the "all means of grace, the word and sacraments" as made useable and beneficial by the Christian.

means? The preaching of the Word, the administration of the sacraments, church discipline, *etc.* These are the "means of salvation and of further sanctification." These are the means of salvation (justification), and being made more holy (sanctification). All the means of grace are centered around Jesus Christ, his work, his death, his resurrection, his ascension and his present intercession. Whether looking forward to Christ coming as Jeremiah did, or looking back to the cross and resurrection as Christians have done for 2000 years, the means of grace includes everything which communicates biblical light and truth, to lead resolute believers to heed it and rightly exercise themselves in it by the power of the Spirit.

In the Old Testament, before the death of Christ in actual time, this properly belonged to the sacrificial system and the temple, performed by the priests. By *faith* men trusted in what God had given them as a means to point towards the coming of the Messiah in what *he will do* in deliverance from its types and shadows. But oftentimes, men sinned against these means, not using them as God intended.

After the death of Christ, history points *back* to what the Messiah fulfilled and accomplished for the people of God in his work. This is why you hear that saying of old – there is no salvation outside the church. There is no salvation *outside the means of grace.* This is why it is imperative for converted sinners to invite unconverted sinners *to* the means of grace in a bible-believing church – they must be under the ministry of the word if they are to be converted. But when the means of grace are abused, *salvation* is hard to see in the church; it becomes eclipsed by sin in *many* ways.

Just as God had given the Israelites the temple, with all its rites and sacrifices, yet, they misused it. It couldn't merely be a duty performed. Duties can be good, but they have to be used "well," which means, by the power of the Spirit indwelling believers. It is not just the act of reading the Bible and passing the words over the eyes as the Christian has his daily devotions that are spiritually beneficial. Demons can read a bible. There must be something more. Judah did what they had to do but did it carelessly. That is actually, soul-destroying. These verses reside in the context of a people lost and apostate. They trusted in things, and not in God.

Can this truth be seen, that it is a soul-destroying sin applied both directly to the lost and principally to the Christian? Sinning against the means of grace should be considered *generally* here. It greatly *aggravates sin*. I only make mention of this because sinning against the means of grace is different than having a bad record and a bad heart. Fallen men and women are *fallen*. They have a bad record and a bad heart on account of Adam. They are fallen in sin, and then they further aggravate that original imputed sin by acting out all kinds of "aggravations" of that sin. They sin in everything they do, with depravity of mind that is total. But there is a degree of difference between the Aborigine who sins with his fallen heart in worshipping an idol who may have never heard the Gospel, and the one who has the means of grace who sins against God in it because they misuse it. More light equals more responsibility. In both the Old Testament and the New Testament God commands repentance and faith in the Messiah, in Jesus Christ, in his Branch, in his Rod, in his righteous Servant, or one *cannot* be spiritually useful in God's kingdom. However, under the New Testament, faith is no longer hid in shadows and types. It is more plainly pressed so that sinners can believe in the Lord Jesus Christ *who came*, not the Messiah who still needs to come. The *extent* of perceived grace given in the New Testament is greater – far more light is, in fact, *more* light. Unbelief, then, is *more* clearly and severely threatened. So, when people say that they go to church, they read their bible, they pray, they do such and such around various ordinances of God, when they sin against those means of grace in ignorance or indifference, it adds a far greater aggravation than any other sin. Sins either neglecting the means of grace, or sins misusing the means of grace, are extraordinarily heinous in God's sight.

Consider, in what ways do *Christless men* live carelessly before the means of grace? First, as the text primarily demonstrates, men assume that because they *have* the means of grace that they will be saved. This *is* living carelessly before the means of grace. Utter folly! This is one of the greatest satanic attacks on the blinded mind of lost men. Some *form* of religiosity, some form of duty, some attachment to the things of God, in no way qualifies one as converted...ever! Possession of the means does not render a man by default, one who has *obtained the grace that the means offers*. Think about verse 4! "Trust not in lying words saying the temple of the Lord..." Just because a man may purchase a bible in Wal-Mart does not mean that gives him an instantaneous ticket to heaven, though many people *think in that line of thought*. God must effectually qualify those means in the hearts of men by his Spirit; otherwise men cry out "we have the temple, I go to church, I pray, I read my bible...and so everything will be just fine."

Second, the lost trust in the means and not the God of the means. This is living carelessly before the means of grace. They do not listen to the words, "Trust ye not in lying words..." They trust in the *possibility* of the spiritual reality which becomes carnal, and wicked, and discards the truth of means. It becomes twisted knowledge by the fallen mind and carnal heart. They take that which could be a means to salvation, and strip it of its power.[44] It becomes a duty that they achieve and that they perform in some legalistic manner, and that they work for, and the spiritual means of grace becomes a carnal medium to satisfy their fallen conscience. It makes them feel good to do it; and that's about all. Ultimately these kinds of people become exceedingly miserable because there is really nothing going on

---

[44] "Having a form of godliness, but denying the power thereof," (2 Tim. 3:5).

except a form of *carnal habit*, a *form* of godliness while denying its *power*. There is no transformation, no sanctification, no real attainment of a living relationship with the Lord's Christ; how long can such a thing really last? They have a *form of godliness* but deny its real power because *they* become its power in their own actions, instead of submitting to God through his word by his Spirit for the glory of Christ. Churches all across the Bible-belt where I personally live, are filled with these kinds of people. They go to church because their parents went there, or their grandparents, and so they do the same. They do it because it's part of their *heritage*. But this, by no means, guarantees them a place in heaven, though, at funerals, everyone thinks everyone in the church has made it to heaven.

      Third, the lost also trust in a false application of the knowledge of the means of grace, and the experience of those means. This is also living carelessly before the means of grace. The Jews knew their duty; they knew what had to be done in the temple – the meticulous obedience to the letter of the law – and yet, not the spirit of the law. What could the Jews have gained if, after they had sacrificed in the temple, they had to go to Baal and worship there, or sacrificed some children to the god Molech? Or simply just wandered into church because it was the day to hear a sermon from the preacher? Religious men may be exceedingly meticulous about their religiosity, but in doing so, they *forfeit* the means of grace if Christ is not attached to it. A Christless soul in attending a church service (a *great* means of grace) could be exceedingly diligent to be on time and take their seat, participate thoroughly in song, take notes diligently, not miss one iota of the sermon, while all the while miss the entire means of grace! They do it all as a legalistic duty instead of a means to receive more of Jesus Christ in godly obedience. Judas did this. Judah did this.

How do *Christians* live carelessly before the means of grace? Saved believers have been converted, qualified by the sanctifying effect of the Spirit, and made alive through the one and only Messiah Jesus Christ, bought with the infinite price of Christ's sacrifice, converted and underneath the blood of the everlasting covenant. They are sons and daughters of priceless grace. Certainly, *they* can't live carelessly before the means of grace, can they? The people of Judah, for all intents and purposes were the "Christians" of the narrative. They weren't the Philistines, or the Babylonians, or the Assyrians. They had the temple, the temple of the Lord, the temple of the Lord.

The first way Christians can live carelessly before the means of grace is because they *have* the means of grace, they believe they are sanctified whenever they use or attend them. These means are accessible – and they have been enlightened to realize their importance. But many times, they think, that simply because they *had their devotions today*, that it automatically sanctifies them further just by the very fact *that they had them*. They may even think that by having one, or two, or three devotions each day that somehow, God automatically attends the duty of reading, or study or prayer, and the like. That the exercised *duty* sanctifies them. This does not mean that such duties are not sanctifying if they are used rightly in the Spirit, but they are not necessarily used *rightly* even when they are used...as much as the temple was.

Secondly, they misuse grace by neglecting the means of sanctifying grace. Christians truly know that morning devotions will be a help to their souls, it will edify them, and strengthen them, *etc*. It has happened to them before because God has blessed his divine works *in their exercise* – but if they are neglected, they won't be of any use. They may engage in short devotions, because they think "some devotion" is better than none. They may be too tired, which is often a hindrance. They might be too tired to have devotions, to attend prayer meeting (or to pray at the meeting), to conduct family devotions, to read their bible, to study, to memorize verses, *etc*. They have had a long day, and are worn out; they have had a busy day and are exhausted; or, they give God their "dopey time" when they are not thinking well. Devotions like this become forced into a duty in these instances. "My duty has been done for the day! I got through it!" They think all is well because they went through the motions.

Thirdly, they mistakenly look at the means as a duty and not as a means to reach their blessed Savior. Many find reading the bible a drudgery. They say to themselves, "I'm in Numbers, I'm in Chronicles. I don't understand what I'm reading, *etc.*" The Christian should not think of their Bible reading as drudgery, but as a love letter sent to them by Christ. When they don't, that is part of living carelessly! Though the means are in their grasp, and though they use them, it doesn't necessarily mean the *way* they use these means is of God's order and directive. God gives certain directions to using the means of grace. But there are two problems with the way Christians use them. First is their *preparation* to use them. How do they think about devotions, or hearing the word preached, or singing out loud? Second, is their execution in using them. How *well* do they read, or listen, or sing?

Fourthly, if they do utilize some of the means of grace, and they use them properly, they are content with being *a little sanctified.* This is often a great hindrance and using the means of grace carelessly. There is not a violence in *taking* the Kingdom of heaven and pressing into it with hearty resolve. There is a lack of zeal. There is a lack of earnestness. There is enough to keep them going, but not growing. God says that if the Christian becomes serious about the means he has given them, that he will cause them to "dwell," (verse 3 of the text). But dwell where? Dwelling *with God* is the Christian's delight. This is where Christ takes the serious Christian seriously. Those Christians that have a desire to live whole-heartedly before Christ with a biblical resolve will be, by promise, blessed by God to live in such a manner. After a single taste of such help, they would never settle for being just a little sanctified.

By way of notation, the saint that uses the means well, even in a shorter time, will reap more of a benefit that the busied saint that gains little from their misuse of the means though they have five devotions a day. Abraham Lincoln debated Stephen Douglas for the Presidency in his day. Lincoln spoke 2 minutes, and Douglas spoke 2 hours. Lincoln won, and Douglas after said to him, "I wished I could have said what you said in two minutes than what I did in my two hours." The grasp on elocution in this way allowed Lincoln to get the point across in a more meaningful manner than with the barrage of words and time it took Douglas to blow it. There is truth to this as it applies to the means of grace. The barrage of material or time or study that sometimes goes into it is not effective because such time is not used wisely, which often results in burnout. "Of making many books there is no end, and much study is wearisome to the flesh," (Eccl. 12:12). Much study can be wearisome. It is the difference between spraying the battlefield field with bullets hoping to hit the target, and the sniper who strikes his mark in a shot or two. One must not drink from a firehose, but a water fountain.

For the resolute Christian who wants to use the means of grace sincerely, and with spiritual benefit, they know it is a soul-destroying sin and a hindrance to sanctification to live carelessly before God's ordained means of grace.

Mark 4: Resolved to Righteously Use the Means of Grace

When we speak about the means of grace, we are talking about those institutions which God has ordained to be the ordinary channels of grace *to you*. They are the supernatural influences of the Holy Spirit in the preaching and reading of the word, the right administration of the sacraments, and the uses of prayer and godly meditation. We are not speaking about various providences that God uses in our lives. The Bible teaches that the word, sacraments and prayer are the specific means God uses to affect our growth. How well are such things used by you? Not only used, but *used well?*

If you thought of one person in the Bible who was exposed to the means of grace more than any other, and did not use it meaningfully, who would that be? It could be a few choices – but I would pick Judas. You may be like Judas. Remember, Judas heard all of Christ's sermons, did miracles, walked with Christ for three years, prayed with him, read the scriptures with him, was sent out and preached for him, was immersed, so to speak, in religion *with the Savior*, and ultimately, the world choked him. It is a perversion of the means of grace to live carelessly under them. A banquet is prepared, but instead of resolving to eat heartily at the feast, you have a food fight. You take the means and carelessly abuse them. The Jews were sent into exile for their sin, and a much worse fate is reserved for all those who abuse the means of grace in hell.

Avoid soul-destroying sins. Oftentimes we think that sins which hurt us are things that go directly against God's Moral Law. Lying, murder, adultery and the like (sins we think are big). Would you have ever placed *reading God's word poorly* as a soul-destroying sin and a misuse of the means of grace? Or *shallow prayers* as a soul-destroying sin? Would you have ever placed *cold prayers* as a soul-destroying sin and a misuse of the means of grace? Would you have placed the *neglect of meditating on the word of God* a soul-destroying sin and neglect of the means of grace?

It is a soul-destroying sin not to make *a good use* of the means of grace. Attending on God's ordinances is *commanded*. Using the means of grace is *required*. Such spiritual benefits have been provided by God's Christ for your good. So, consider, at what point in your Christian walk will you prepare and use them perfectly in this life? Will that happen at any time? No, unfortunately there will never be a time when you use them *perfectly*. In that concept alone you are to *covet them* in such a way as to desire their use *to the best of your ability by employing every duty in the blood of Christ, by the power of the Spirit*. What you deem perfect, good, the best, and the like, can also be a hindrance to even using them. "I don't pray well so I'm not going to pray. I don't feel as though I read very well, so I'm not going to read. I don't feel as though I'm ready to hear the word preached, so I'm not going to church. I had bad thoughts this past day, and didn't mortify them well, and so, I can't come to the throne of grace to pray well before the Lord." Those kinds of arguments can be extremely hindering to your soul's growth. That is a form of legalism (working for salvation). It is always a hindrance and never a help to think that you are the power behind your use of the means of grace. *Not using* the means of grace is sin. The logic you might have in thinking, "unless I prepare my heart to pray well, then I'm not praying," is a false conclusion to the use of the means. The problem is that when you engage in these things, you are trying to come based on your own strength, (I, I, I) and that will never do. You must come bringing Christ with you; always take Christ to everything. You must always look to God through Christ the Mediator, otherwise God will never be sweet and delightful to you, but always a hard Judge.

Instead, use the means of grace by the Spirit's power.[45] When your inward corruption and remaining sin prevails over you, it makes you unprofitable. It then makes your attempt at benefitting from the means of grace, unprofitable as well. It hardens your heart, and you come to prayer, you come to hear the word, and you come to partake of the Lord's Supper, and you find little to no benefit. Is that God's fault or your fault? You complain that you are not growing as you would like in Christ, that you do not experience a full benefit of his love to you, or that you do not profit by prayer, hearing the word, and have no real sense of Christ' work on your

---

[45] See my work, *Walking Victoriously in the Power of the Spirit* for a full treatment of this kind of walking.

heart when you take the sacrament of the Lord's Supper. Why? Is God responsible? No, it is because you are misusing the means. So, don't wonder why you do not profit as you desire, or grow from week to week, or month to month. The answer is relatively easy. You may simply be coming to the means of grace in the wrong way; without the help of Jesus. It shows us that we must use our heart as well as our head. It is not simply that we know it, but that we must do it, and do it well in his power and Spirit because *we love him and love the means of grace for our spiritual good.*

In all the means God has given us, we must take advantage to walk according to the rule of the divine word. God has given us certain means which are at our fingertips if we would simply put them, not to *use*, but to *good use*. Bible reading, daily prayer, daily meditation on the word, family worship, reading good books, the blessed spiritual rest of the Lord's Day, church and all its service to our soul, are all helps for us. Is God content with your level of spirituality? If he is not, why would *you* be? And if you aren't, why are you not taking more keen advantage of the means he has provided for your spiritual growth? Never neglect them. Sin must never throw you off taking advantage of those means; be resolved to walk heartily with Christ and his Spirit in his ordained means.

With all the wealth of knowledge we have in our day how could we ever neglect the means of sanctifying grace? Then the question arises, why are we not spiritual giants? Why do we need to look *back* in history to find spiritual giants? With thousands of professing "reformed churches" all over the United States, why is it that no one is saying, "They who have turned the world upside down have come here as well?" We are not spiritual giants because we *misuse* the means of grace. We tend to be satisfied with *just a little*. Are the means of grace any different from the time of the Reformation than they are now? Are we really that tired in our walk with Christ to devote ourselves to him in such a weak measure? We may be *doing* much, but we may be mishandling such things if we are not constantly growing in grace. How could we ever be tired to obey Christ in the means with which the Spirit of God would sanctify us further? Why don't we see that as vitally important? Why isn't that part of our church prayer list?

Judah *did not hear* Jeremiah; may we hear him? We act foolishly when we neglect the means used rightly that will furnish us with eternal life. It is where we place duty against delight. We might do more, but out of compulsion. Grace does not come in tidal waves simply because you shout, "I have the temple of the Lord," a few times. It is firmly set in the spiritual resolve.

Lastly, consider the benefits of rightly attending the means of grace. We obtain salvation, more of Jesus Christ, when we use his means rightly. "I will cause you to dwell," God says. Drawing near, dwelling, being close to God is our desire (or it should be). Neglect the means of grace, and you cast God aside. The means of grace are pathways to Jesus. They are cell phone connections to him each time we use them. We make a call to him, and we get a two-way connection; us to him, and him to us. Some means are more visible and special, like the preached word, or the Lord's Supper, but all are a communication of grace to the soul. We obtain grace in them; we obtain more of Jesus. In this sanctifying influence, God attends us when we attend him. We obtain sanctification, conformed to Jesus Christ. God makes us more holy when we attend on those means he has given us if use them rightly. Not simply saying we go to church, but that we heed what we learn. It is never perfect, but it will always be helpful if we bring Christ along with us.

We use them rightly when we use them as often as we can with gravity and consideration, with a hearty resolve and resolution to suck the virtue out of Christ for the good of our soul. Use them as God directs us. Use them zealously. Use them bringing Christ, and in reliance on the Spirit.

Examine your own seriousness in these things today. Did you prepare your heart for the Lord's Day service last week? Did you prepare the night before to be well rested? Did *you* prepare in your own strength, or did *God prepare you in the power of the Spirit?* Do you see the difference in that? Don't be content simply to check *church* off your list of good things you think you have done this week. Judah did just that, and lived carelessly before the means of grace. They did things because they ... *did things*. They had the temple, they had the priesthood, they had the means of grace, but they did not use them well, using them in righteous truth and with great delight in the promise of the Messiah by the power of his gracious Spirit.

Other than the allusion to "the making of books" in Ecclesiastes, and our text for this part of the study, there was not mentioned a single other Scripture in this whole chapter. Why? Because Jeremiah 7 was enough to get the point across. Be resolved *never* to live carelessly before God's means of grace. Never abuse them, never neglect them. May we all consider the gravity of the statement, that it is soul-destroying sin to live carelessly neglecting or misusing the means of grace. Instead, be resolved to serve the living Christ all the days of your life for his glory.

MARK 5: Resolved to Continue to Do Good

"Let him that is taught in the word communicate unto him that teacheth in all good things. Be not deceived; God is not mocked: for whatsoever a man soweth, that shall he also reap. For he that soweth to his flesh shall of the flesh reap corruption; but he that soweth to the Spirit shall of the Spirit reap life everlasting. And let us not be weary in well doing: for in due season we shall reap, if we faint not. As we have therefore opportunity, let us do good unto all men, especially unto them who are of the household of faith," (Gal. 6:6-10).

The work of *doing good continually* is the last mark of a resolute Christian. There are some inquiries to make into the reasons why some become weary in the service of Christ, and there are some suggestions for remedy, as well as a demonstration and exhortation to those opposed to any good work.

In considering this Galatian text, I give you only some brief contextual considerations. The Apostle Paul writes to a church in Galatia, which it seemed there were many in various cities in that region. They were needing specific doctrinal direction, lest they be pulled away to *another Gospel*. That would be a waste of both time and effort, and spiritually detrimental to them. Paul desired to correct them with the soundness of the Gospel of Jesus Christ. That which he preached before to them concerning the kingdom of God, and the Christ who sits upon the throne of God. The apostle's object in the Epistle is to recall the Galatians to the gospel which they had at the first received from himself—the unchangeable gospel of justification by the free grace of God, simply through faith in Christ, and not by deeds of the Law.

The verses are set within concluding remarks, which centers on verse 2. "Bear one another's burdens, and so fulfill the law of Christ," (Gal. 6:2). In other words, as serving the great King of heaven, listen to his law, and love one another (speaking to the second table of the Moral Law). The generality of bearing one another's burdens sets the stage in verses 2-5. Everyone is to pull their own weight together in the church and work from a disposition of love to the glory of God.

"Let him who is taught the word share in all good things with him who teaches," (Gal. 6:6). He exhorts the Galatian Christians to support pastors and teachers in the church in verse 6 (specifically) and not to deride them. Those who are being taught the word of God are to share in common, things that would be beneficial to those who are taking up teaching in the church. Why? Teaching takes study and study takes time and time takes away from one's livelihood in having to make sermon preparation, especially for these newly planted churches with bi-vocational pastors. Therefore, these teachers would have need to be supported by the church, and so pastoral support was very important.

Otherwise the work of the Gospel would instantly cease. There must be some proper form of instruction in the church, and those instructing are to be supported *by* the church, as much as God would providentially bless them in such an endeavor. These Galatian Christians (if necessity requires) make those that *instruct* partakers of "all their goods," (Gal. 6:6). This is not just speaking of the natural response of giving as in Genesis 14 with Abraham to Melchizedek before the Law, but to such a supply, as that God's worship may be upheld in the church through their support. How will the church continue in its Gospel proclamation unless the church is financially sustained?

    Was there a failure to distinguish between the support of godly preachers, which Paul previous speaks about in chapter 1? There is a need to support both preachers and teachers seen in Galatians 1:6-8. It seems the Galatian Christians were confused about how to deal with the primitive church in recognizing the role of teachers. Paul in Galatians 1 speaks about preachers who preach erroneous Gospels, and those, here in the text, that teach or catechize those in the church righteously. There is a great difference between them, but the false teachers, the wayward teachers would cause spiritual *harm* to the church.

    There seemed to be, overall, a failure to act in supporting the Gospel preacher. They were not to believe any other Gospel than the one preached to them by Paul, and they were to support *those* preaching the truth.

"Do not be deceived, God is not mocked; for whatever a man sows, that he will also reap. For he who sows to his flesh will of the flesh reap corruption, but he who sows to the Spirit will of the Spirit reap everlasting life," (Gal. 6:7-8). There was also a failure to understand. God will not bless such false teaching and the sowing of false doctrine. Large churches with many teachers are *not* a sign of prosperity. When false doctrine comes into the church, regardless of its outward prosperity, (for many false teachers or bad teachers can huddle around them many itching ears to hear), there is given by God a negative promise. "Do not be deceived, God is not mocked; for whatever a man sows, that he will also reap," (Gal. 6:7). Mocking God is actually to despise his ways with one's whole being. Sowing in destruction, sowing in false doctrine, sowing in wayward teaching is akin to mocking God. Believe something false and God is mocked.[46] God has given the truth, why would these Galatians be drawn away into something *other* than the truth? Paul instructs them to sow into the teaching function of the church, and they will reap benefits by this, (verse 8).

Will these Christians support a false Gospel, or godly teachers in the church? What will they receive

---

[46] "But they mocked the messengers of God, and despised his words, and misused his prophets, until the wrath of the LORD arose against his people, till there was no remedy," (2 Chron. 36:16).

from false teachers but being thrown off the path of salvation? Paul says in 2 Tim. 2:17, "their message will spread like cancer..." Their message will spread like disease, death and destruction.

In opposition to being carried away by false teaching, they are to support the truth, and truth's teachers. What will they receive from *them?* The church teacher is a merchant of the most valuable jewels of Jesus Christ.[47] Ministers to Christ's church are called angels.[48] They are very important because they are the heralds of God's word and act as God's mouthpiece.[49] There are far too many Scriptures to deal with on the value of what they bring if they preach boldly, plainly and faithfully. Conversion, salvation, wisdom, hope, obedience, cleansing, comfort, admonishment, rejoicing, delight in Jesus Christ the Mediator of the covenant, *etc.*

In essence, these Galatians are supporting either heaven or hell; sowing destruction or sowing to eternal life. "For he who sows to his flesh will of the flesh reap corruption, but he who sows to the Spirit will of the Spirit reap everlasting life," (Gal. 6:8). To persevere in doing what is good and supporting what is good is to hold to the truth and "sow to the Spirit." Those who do

---

[47] "Who, when he had found one pearl of great price, went and sold all that he had, and bought it," (Matt. 13:46). "...that I should preach among the Gentiles the unsearchable riches of Christ," (Eph. 3:8).
[48] "Unto the angel of the church of Ephesus write," (Rev. 2:1).
[49] "If there be a messenger with him, an interpreter, one among a thousand, to shew unto man his uprightness," (Job. 33:23). "The LORD'S voice crieth unto the city, and the man of wisdom shall see thy name: hear ye the rod, and who hath appointed it," (Micah 6:9).

so without growing faint will reap a harvest in time. This will be his exhortation. People always exemplify where they are going (heaven or hell) by what they say and what they do; especially where they desire to place their finances and goods. Jesus made this very simple when he said, "A tree is known by its fruit."[50] The fruit does not make a tree good or bad, the fruit merely tells us whether the tree is a good tree or bad tree. Tally up whatever doctrine someone teaches, and place it up against the historical veracity of the church and you find out very quickly whether they are in good company, or whether they are leading their people astray into some strange doctrine. Paul was worried that these Galatians might be pouring themselves into support for those who do not teach and preach the true Gospel.[51]

"And let us not grow weary while doing good, for in due season we shall reap if we do not lose heart," (Gal. 6:9). Paul commands from the specific to the general. From catechists under teachers, from those learning under ministers, to everyone; then from everyone to the household of faith. The pattern and the precept are given. In the structure of the Greek text, it is what we

---

[50] "For every tree is known by his own fruit. For of thorns men do not gather figs, nor of a bramble bush gather they grapes. A good man out of the good treasure of his heart bringeth forth that which is good; and an evil man out of the evil treasure of his heart bringeth forth that which is evil: for of the abundance of the heart his mouth speaketh. And why call ye me, Lord, Lord, and do not the things which I say?" (Luke 6:44-46).

[51] This is why historical theology is very important. It teaches a Christian consensus on the truth, who deviated from that truth, why they did so, and who fought for the truth against them.

call a *synonymous parallelism*, but the whole paragraph is engulfed in it! It is a literary device used by the Apostle to parallel ideas, and place a great amount of emphasis on those ideas by building them up next to each other. Learners and teachers are included, as well as to Christians supporting one another in every good work.

What was it that he did not want the people to neglect? Overall, these things stretch into pattern and precept of *doing* good; these are things that are good, commendable or excellent to everyone. In this case, Paul is aiming at those *in the church*. These are things that are like God, that reflect his character. He uses a strange phrase, the *weariness of it all* – "do not grow weary," "let us not grow weary while doing good, for in due season we shall reap if we do not lose heart," (Gal. 6:9). Do not become utterly spiritless, and spiritually exhausted. This is a military idea of the militia going to battle tired and spiritless. This is likened to those who would in fact do good but not see the fruit of the good work as instantaneously as they would like and become spiritless in the work itself as a result. Don't grow weary in sowing. Sowing is not reaping. He is exhorting them that time breeds patience, and patiently expect to see what will grow from what is sown. This is not instantaneous. It may take some patience to endure the time it takes.

"Therefore, as we have opportunity, let us do good to all, especially to those who are of the household of faith," (Gal. 6:10). What is "doing good" specifically?

These are individual acts of moral and spiritual goodness to other people. It is fulfilling the *Law of Christ* to all men. It is fulfilling the Law of Christ to the household of faith. It is loving the brethren and doing good to the brethren in order to support the Gospel, to support ministers, to extend that generosity to one another, to support the household of faith. Paul now gives the promise in Gal. 6:9, "In due season we shall reap if we faint not." There is warning though, read into this promise: becoming weary in the work of the Lord may cause the Galatians to faint, grow weary, and stop their ministry. If they faint, they will reap little to nothing. There is a Greek nuance in this verse worth noting. We see "as we have opportunity," which can be translated as "*while* we have opportunity." This does not *change* the command, but it does set it in a context of *warning*. There may be a time, you Galatian Christians, where you will have *no opportunity*. There may be a time when opportunity has *escaped you*. So, take advantage at every opportunity, instead of inwardly fighting and quarreling. Instead, be sowing to the Spirit, to the truth, and to the good of the church. The *household of faith* is a first concern, and an ultimate concern in this.

What is the "household of faith?" In Christ, Christian service lays the best and only foundation for true friendship. In the household of faith, among believers *united* to the truth, friends may be formed, and the most endearing and happy friendships are cultivated. There is a peculiar friendship between

Christians. They love one another with a peculiar love of benevolence and complacency. They are disposed, as they are commanded, to acts of kindness to the household of faith, and this *specially*, in *the first place*, which is the meaning of Gal. 6:10. Those Galatians who are most acquainted with each other will exercise and enjoy this friendship to a much higher degree. They take a particular pleasure in conversing with each other. They put great confidence in each other. They exercise doing good to each other, and praying for one another, and expressing their love and friendship in all the proper ways that they should. James Ussher said, "We must prefer those that are of the household of faith before others."[52] It is there that the precept lies – doing good *especially to the household of faith.*

    Consider also, in Paul's command, unless the Galatian Christians can discern *who are of* the household of faith, there is the impossibility of being able to do them good. It certainly is not directed to false teachers, but true teachers, true Christians, or Gospel teachers. *Gospelers* all around. There must be, then, some measure of accountability to one another in the household *in order to* do them good. This text argues greatly for why covenanted membership in a church is of great importance. Without such, without knowing who such people are, it is not possible to fulfill the command as it is instructed to do good especially to these people. Paul does not say to the Galatians, "do good to those you

---

[52] Ussher, James, *A Body of Divinitie*, (London: M.F., 1645), 255.

judge to do good to." He gives them a discerning eye to do good *to the household of faith.* And it is not about, simply, people who *attend* a church, but it is more particular of those who *belong* to God's house. When one goes from house to house, there are people who live in that house, who own the house, who manage the house; and the church is seen in this same light.

This household is the depository of all the benefits of Jesus Christ to his people, and it must be discerned.[53] It is not simply people who *attend* a church. It is not simply people in a community. It is specifically those who are beneficiaries of Christ's grace. The public proclamation of such people in the eyes of others and in covenant with the church demonstrates they belong to something. These, especially, are those to whom good is to be done according to the Apostle.

Make a note, that true godliness is more than a whim. Time is a great winnower. Chaff and wheat are winnowed with a winnowing fork – they are separated. Time often has a habit of winnowing out those who are truly converted and knee deep in the battle, and those who are just professing to be part of the battle, looking only to wear the uniform of Christ's army. Time will indeed separate such, one from another.

Godliness before the Lord Jesus Christ is also more than a whim. Doing good to the household of faith

---

[53] "In whom are hid all the treasures of wisdom and knowledge," (Col. 2:3). "...nor trust in uncertain riches, but in the living God, who giveth us richly all things to enjoy," (1 Tim. 6:17). "If thou seekest her as silver, and searchest for her as for hid treasures," (Pro. 2:4).

demonstrates itself in many ways, the difference between hypocritical Christians and Christians engaging in true holiness in the power of the Spirit, by sowing in the Spirit. So, the doctrine to consider here is that: Christians are commanded to persevere, and not to grow weary in doing good especially to the household of faith.

    Yes, they are commanded to do good, to be resolved in doing good *no matter what.* But, this is a strange command indeed. Is there really weariness in serving Christ? Weariness in serving God? Is it tiresome to serve God? In point of fact, yes, it is, when fallen people become part of the factor. It is service to God in a fallen world riddled with sin among fallen people who do not act like Christians all the time. Or do not know how to act like Christians because they may have never been taught. But, it is a realistic command in this present evil age for the Christian to waste no time, and fully commit to sowing a harvest with his whole life. Biblical religion is the Christian's business. Christians are on the highway of holiness to serve Christ while on earth living among God's people. Every office and station in the church is an office and station of *service.*[54] And not only

---

[54] "With good will doing service, as to the Lord, and not to men," (Eph. 6:7). "Yea, and if I be offered upon the sacrifice and service of your faith, I joy, and rejoice with you all," (Phil. 2:17). "I know thy works, and charity, and service, and faith, and thy patience, and thy works; and the last to be more than the first," (Rev. 2:19).

service, but a *persevering service*.⁵⁵ It is patient continuance and perseverance in well-doing.⁵⁶ Abounding in good works, filled with the fruit of all righteousness.⁵⁷ This is a striving towards *perfecting* holiness and having works *full* before the face of God. Increasing so that their last works may be better than their first works. Doing everything without weariness; without dismay and fainting, notwithstanding all hindrances. This can be a very tough task in not growing weary.

Why should Christians do this? So that Christians may escape fearful apostasy, for such works demonstrate *the general precepts of a holy life*.⁵⁸ "...perfecting holiness in the fear of God," (2 Cor. 7:1). Godly diligence is often a cure for spiritual declension. In the Christian walk, Christians are either moving forward or backward. Don't be deceived – Christianity is *never* neutral. Either the Christian is advancing, or he is retreating. The idea of standing still is simply an

---

⁵⁵ "I beseech you therefore, brethren, by the mercies of God, that ye present your bodies a living sacrifice, holy, acceptable unto God, which is your reasonable service," (Rom. 12:1).
⁵⁶ "But let patience have her perfect work, that ye may be perfect and entire, wanting nothing," (James 1:4).
⁵⁷ "...it yieldeth the peaceable fruit of righteousness unto them which are exercised thereby," (Heb. 12:11).
⁵⁸ "For we are his workmanship, created in Christ Jesus unto good works, which God hath before ordained that we should walk in them," (Eph. 2:10). "That they do good, that they be rich in good works," (1 Tim. 6:18). "...they may by your good works, which they shall behold, glorify God in the day of visitation," (1 Peter 2:12). "And let us consider one another to provoke unto love and to good works," (Heb. 10:24).

illusion. One is either moving forward in the Spirit and sowing to the Spirit, or they are sowing to the flesh and walking with sin. There are no Scriptures for Christians to be *idle*. Press into the Kingdom,[59] take the kingdom with violence, be the knight who besieges the castle, striving to enter into the Kingdom.[60] Christians are to labor after this kind of service, if they intend to be like God, or to manifest his glory in their lives to the world. It is a work of holiness.[61] When men live to themselves, and are satisfied that they are relatively good people, and don't hurt anyone, even though they do not do anything *good* as defined by God, they become carnally secure, selfish, wrathful, angry, *etc.*, and there is with them no usefulness in Christ's kingdom.[62]

Christians must look to this kind of well-doing, doing good, as a kind of holy service to Jesus Christ. If they desire to be holy, they should constantly look to be like God in his kindness and benevolence. They labor to be conformed by the renewing of their mind which is their *spiritual act of service*, to labor after imitating God as dear children (Eph. 5:1). God is philanthropic, good, kind, condescending to save, ready to forgive, ready to help, ready to relive all sinful distresses in and through Jesus Christ. If people do not wish to be like him, they

---

[59] "...the kingdom of heaven suffereth violence, and the violent take it by force," (Matt. 11:12).
[60] "Strive to enter in at the strait gate," (Luke 13:24).
[61] "Whereunto I also labour, striving according to his working, which worketh in me mightily," (Col. 1:29).
[62] "And cast ye the unprofitable servant into outer darkness," (Matt. 25:30).

demonstrate they are not his children. God's children are especially suited by the fruit of the Spirit to act in accordance with this special nature of God's kindness in Christian service. "For the kingdom of God is not meat and drink; but righteousness, and peace, and joy in the Holy Ghost," (Rom. 14:17).

Christians ought to be steeped in persevering service to believers. It is true, they are to help the poor, be at peace with all men, love their enemies and the like, which are all important commands as they live in the world. But they are *especially* to be mindful of the household of saints, *the church*. To, "the least of these my brethren," (Matt. 25:40). God himself, whom Christians are to imitate and conform to in Christ's actions, exercises his kindness in a peculiar manner towards the church. 1 Tim. 4:10, "He is the Savior of all men, but especially of them that believe." There is a specialty in his exercise of saving goodness towards believers. This is why the Apostle says here, "to do good unto all men, but *especially* to them who are of the household of faith," (Gal. 6:10). Although Christians are obliged to exercise goodness to all men whoever they might be, even to love their enemies,[63] as they have opportunity, they are particularly joined to that special

---

[63] "But I say unto you, Love your enemies, bless them that curse you, do good to them that hate you, and pray for them which despitefully use you, and persecute you; That ye may be the children of your Father which is in heaven: for he maketh his sun to rise on the evil and on the good, and sendeth rain on the just and on the unjust," (Matt. 5:44-45).

regard of Christians in the household of faith. Imagine if Christians felt obliged to be kind in all their dealings with others in the church all the time? How many offenses and animosities would the simple act of love overcome? Love covers over a multitude of sins.[64] This is a reason why Christ says that Pharisees and publicans love their own, because its relatively easy to love people you, well, *love*. Serve those that are *not easy to serve*. Serve for the sake of *being like Christ to the unlovely*. Christians are to conform to Christ and God, mimicking goodness with perseverance regardless of the return they think they are owed. They do it, because it is God's will.

    Christians have strength to do good. In doing good, Christians are to rely on Jesus Christ, the supreme and sovereign God of the universe who supplies his people with the power to overcome through the Spirit. Sow good works *in the Spirit*. The intercession of Jesus Christ, which is contrary to the false Gospel Paul warned Christians of in Galatians 1, is to be resolved to fight with the jawbone of Christ's victory in the power of the Spirit. This requires in the Christian a steadfast *resolution* to walk in the Spirit sent by Jesus Christ. It is walking in the light with him in fellowship (1 John 1:7-10). It is walking to serve. Christ secured such a walk by His covenant, perfect obedience, death, resurrection and intercession for *all* Christians. All authority is Christ's –

---

[64] "And above all things have fervent charity among yourselves: for charity shall cover the multitude of sins," (1 Peter 4:8).

and so, Christians should be of good cheer for he has given such eminent power in the Spirit to those who seek and resolve to do good. He will cause them to mount up with wings as eagles, to run, and not to become faint. Not only is the power given to enact the good work, but every opportunity is sovereignly placed before every Christian by the supreme Christ, the great King, sent directly from the throne of God to their present circumstance. Will the Christian recognize that it's there? Thomas Cole, a famous puritan preacher, said "The Christian is never more obliged to their duty, than when they have the fittest opportunity to perform it."[65] When it is right there, sent from Christ, for them to do good, right in front of them, it is a shame if they do not see it. What reason could there be that they do not see what God's endeavoring strength will open up to them? There are many doors to serve him, for serving the church is serving God.

There are great temptations in growing weary. In doing good, there is the temptation to *give into* growing weary. Believers ought to be, "sold out for Christ," some say. But Paul is talking about being *tired* for Christ. Not just getting tired – but becoming lethargic and idle. A little sleep, a little slumber, a little folding of the hands,

---

[65] Cole, Thomas, quoted in James Nichols, *Puritan Sermons*, Vol. 3 (Wheaton, IL: Richard Owen Roberts, Publishers, 1981), 477. Sermon: <u>How may the well-discharge of our present duty give us assurance of help from God for the well-discharge of all future duties?</u>

and the Christian finds himself asleep in some cove called *Ease* on the road of salvation like John Bunyan's Pilgrim. Satan would not so much be the Christian's enemy if God were not so much the Christian's friend. The Christian is directed to pray against "evil" or more literally "the evil one" in the Lord's Prayer. Doing good to the household of faith is the last thing the kingdom of darkness wants to see occur. Satan wants to *stop* that. How much effort must the forces of darkness use against a slumbering Christian who has become weary? Not much really. Christians must overcome the lion of temptation like Samson, who found the next day a nest of sweet honey in the dead carcass of the beast (Judges 14:8). They must overcome the temptation to give up and look forward to the harvest if they *faint not*.[66]

    There are rewards for doing good. Is this appealing to the Christian? Christians will be *rewarded* for persevering. People love rewards. Heaven will be a place made more joyous for each believer as a result of rewards. That means Christians ought to be "up and doing" if they want to reap more of heaven now in them as they serve God on earth, that they may have more of a capacity of happiness in heaven when they enter the pearly gates. Scripture gives numerous examples of reward for the Christian, crowns, blessings, eternal benefits, and such.[67] Things sown at the opportune time

---

[66] "For which cause we faint not," (2 Cor. 4:16).
[67] See Edwards in his Misc. 367 on DEGREES OF GLORY. "Christ by his righteousness purchased for everyone perfect happiness; that is, he merited that their capacity should be filled with happiness.

will later bring reaping. Sowing does not immediately bring fruit; God gives it in his time. This means in doing good, constantly, there is a complete and utter reliance on God's providence, "...as the providence of God does in general reach to all creatures, so after a more special manner it takes care of His church, and disposes of all things to the good thereof," (as the *1647 Westminster Confession of Faith* 5:7 on *Providence* directs). A harvest of good things will in turn occur through Christ's blessing if the Christian perseveres in good works. Not only is the Christian blessed. All those to whom the Christian has sowed will be blessed as well. God will bless *both*. But God does the blessing in his time.

There is the necessity of doing good. As God gives according to the Christian's abilities, they are to be ready to do good. They are to be ready to relieve those that are sick, weak, in need, or in any other observed affliction. "As we have therefore opportunity, let us do good unto all men, especially unto them who are of the household of faith," (Gal. 6:10); *i.e.,* that are of the mind,

---

But this don't hinder but that the saints, being of various capacities, may have various degrees of happiness, and yet all their happiness be the fruit of Christ's purchase." Edwards, Jonathan, The "Miscellanies": vol. 13, *The Works of Jonathan Edwards,* (New Haven; London: Yale University Press, 2002), 437. See also Edward's sermon, *None Are Saved by Their Own Righteousness* where he explains an important distinguishing mark between true striving for grace, from self-righteousness. Edwards, Jonathan, "None Are Saved by Their Own Righteousness," in Sermons and Discourses, 1723–1729, ed. Harry S. Stout and Kenneth P. Minkema, vol. 14, *The Works of Jonathan Edwards*, (New Haven; London: Yale University Press, 1997), 329.

that are children of God, that are of the godly. James tells those who have money to be *ready* to give. It is not enough for the Christian to think about reliving the distress of someone. It is a state of mind. Frequently doing anything encourages habit. It keeps it in the mind and memory. Paul commended the Philippians, that they had, "sent once and again unto his necessity," (Phil. 4:16). He exhorts the Galatians, "not to be weary in well-doing," (Gal. 6:9). Onesiphorus was said to *often refresh* Paul, (2 Tim. 1:16).

    Paul also notes a word of warning in doing good or not doing good. Half a work is not a whole work. It must be a resolute work for God with *all* readiness. Jesus was quite persecuted throughout his ministry, but did not give into weariness. This every Christian ought to consider, "For consider him who endured such hostility from sinners against himself, lest you become weary and discouraged in your souls," (Heb. 12:3). Jesus was *not* wearied in doing good. Doing good must flow everywhere throughout one's life as far as one can manage it in the Spirit's power and direction. Christians may have the ability and power by the Spirit, but they may also require a *further opportunity*. Praying for this will open doors very quickly. John Howe said, "If there is opportunity, let this goodness exert itself; this shall show you a God-like sort of creatures, born of God, bearing his image."[68] Christians must have a resolved

---

[68] Howe, John, *The Works of John Howe*, (New York: E. Sanderson, 1836) 909.

desire to do good to the household of faith, a true and sincere good will to them, a desire to perform towards men what they desire others to perform towards them. And such actions are not empty shows; for hypocrites can do that. Such good will and doing good should be coupled with a declaration of good will in words, actions and duties. This is a great virtue in the believer. Scripture simply calls it *loving our neighbor*.[69] Even in heathen philosophical circles they call it, "humanity." As a note, the opposite of this spiritual virtue of well doing is being selfish. It is described in Scripture as ill-will, envy, grief at the outward blessing of God on others, *self-love*. It is the absence of humility.

You, Christian, are to be about the work of doing good to others. This is a basic disposition of a Christian. You should be filled with a desire for both ability and opportunity to do it. It is true, from a human vantage point, doing good is a difficult work for you since you have to deal with *people*. Yes, people are difficult because people are sinful, and Yes, Christian people are very difficult to deal with too because they have the remnants of remaining sin in them. The farmer's work is difficult – attending the crops until harvest. Baiting the crops, dealing with insects and the like, water and rain, weeds, varmints, too much heat, or too little water. You are the sower. Others are the plants. It takes a great

---

[69] This is attached to the second table of the law by being attached to the first table of the law. *Love God, love your neighbor* is the whole of the Moral Law, on which hang *the whole Scripture*, as Christ says.

amount of effort to sow. And take notice, Paul includes in this work *all* those in the household of faith, not just the people you like, or those you get along with. Christ was always so angry with the Jews who looked inward because he longed for them to reach outward; *reach everyone.* And yet, who yields the crops? As much as you would like instant gratification of your sowing, that is not up to you. It is all part of God's providence, and he is the one who commands the wheels to move here and there and everywhere as in Ezekiel 1 and 10. They go when he wants them to go in his governing providence. They bear fruit when he wants them to bear fruit. God yields the crops – but what a crop it shall be if you do not lose heart! Sometimes sowing into another's life is hard work, and *you don't see* the fruit for many years (or maybe never). But God says *you will reap* a harvest (and you must be satisfied that such a thing might occur when you go to heaven).

Doing good should be your constant work, resolved to serve Christ by serving others. Your Christian service must be as the Old Testament temple's arrangement, it was *without seats.* "Doing" assumes *action* in the opportunity and providence of God. Not doing good is rejecting Christ's good providence. Paul was worried that if they could not do something simple like give a few bucks to support the Gospel, what would they do with their neighbor? It is not good enough to do good for yourself; you must do it to others. Thomas Boston said, "God will never put those away empty from him, that hang on, and will not go without the blessing."[70] Like Jacob wrestling with the angel, "I will not let thee go, except thou bless me," (Gen. 32:26).

Doing good is a rewarding work. Good works will be rewarded. Many Christians really do not understand the balance between being saved by Christ, and engaging in good works. Prov. 13:13 says, "...he who fears the commandment will be rewarded..." How you do this work will be rewarded both in this life and the next. What you sow you reap – there is no biblical statement that says "what you do not sow you do not reap." Again, there is no neutrality for you. You have no neutral in your Christian car, all it has is forward and reverse. God gives you opportunities and abilities to benefit your neighbors, and it ought to be a question to every one of us, what use we have in the world, towards the good of mankind? What benefit do God's people have by us? What advantage do Christ's members receive at our hand? Matthew 25 tells us that this will be a great part of the judgment. "And the King will answer and say to them, "Assuredly, I say to you, inasmuch as you did it to one of the least of these My brethren, you did it to Me,"" (Matt. 25:40). It is interesting that Jesus does not talk about being converted, or believing by faith in his substitutionary atonement, or how the doctrine of God's grace secures the sinner in his book of life (at least not in this passage). When he speaks about rewards and

---

[70] Boston, Thomas, *The Complete Works of Thomas Boston*, Volume 6, (Wheaton: Richard Owen Roberts Publishers, 1980) 352.

judgment, he talks about *doing* things for the good of others.

As a Christian, you are to do good to others in the Spirit – it is his fruit in you after all. You sow in the Spirit, love in the Spirit, worship and rejoice in the Spirit, pray in the Spirit, are renewed in the Spirit, built up together in the Spirit, living, without reservation, in the Spirit, beginning in the Spirit and ending in the Spirit, working in the Spirit, ministering in the Spirit, and purposing in the Spirit with great resolve to constantly, and with all diligence, *persevere in doing good* for the glory of Christ. And this you do to everyone, all men, especially those of the household of faith. What a glorious task is set before you! Certainly, there are myriads of verses for all these points that could be proved out to a great length. All these points deserve books of their own!

God teaches us in this that we are never to be weary of the work God sets us to do. We ought to have great care that furthers the godliness of others as our occasion and ability requires. In this we should be diligent, resolved, and perservingly so. We should not be weary, knowing we work for Christ in this. Did Christ weary in his work? There is a great difference in his life (and yours) between suffering and growing weary. Was he not up for the task? Did he show himself to be a quitter or have a desire to give up? Was he too tired to complete the work that was set before him by the Father? Did he not set himself as an example to all, that you may be imitators of him, following such an example as his? When we do not do good to those around us, we become *thieves* in God's house. We do not sow good things into the people of the church, and instead, we *rob* them of that gift or ability that Christ has given us for them.

It is true, doing good is a dividing work. This is a great *test of works* for religious professors of Christ. People who are really not doing God's work will fail the test. James 2:26, "For as the body without the spirit is dead, so faith without works is dead also." 3 John 1:11, "He that does [what is right] is of God…" In other words, he that does good is of God. He that does not do what is right is not of God. And a person will do nothing at all that is good if they are not *of God.* Matthew Sylvester said, "Will not your crop and harvest be answerable to your seed?"[71] Your outward disposition shows your heart.

The false professor never continues in good works. Bad trees grow rotten fruit. Bad trees *do not* grow good fruit that rots. Bad fruit is in fact *bad fruit.* It's poison. Solomon said in Eccles. 9:10, "All that your hand shall find to do, do it with all your power." Why? For what reason? "For there is neither work, nor invention, nor knowledge, nor wisdom in the grave whither you goest." When you die, time is up! Paul says

---

[71] Sylvester, Matthew, in his Sermon: How we may overcome inordinate love of life and fear of death. Cited in James Nichols, *Puritan Sermons*, Vol. 2, (Wheaton, IL: Richard Owen Roberts, Publishers, 1981), 662.

the same thing in Gal. 6:10, "Do good to all men while you have time." If any of you are able to do any good service either to God's church, or to your neighbor, do it with all speed and with all might, so that death will not rob you of the blessing and reward; and them of the blessing of God.

There are two hindrances to doing good. Sometimes growing weary is a direct result of a lack of devotion to God. Lack of devotions, lack of communion, lack of prayer, lack of involvement in church, lack of fellowship and lack of direction are all on the table to consider. Ask yourself what your communion with God is like. Then ask yourself who has been blessed by your ministry to them. Where has God sent you? To whom have you given a word of encouragement? With whom have you prayed? With whom have you given consolation? Where is the comfort in the words of Scripture from one saint to another? Where is all the good? When devotions fail, your spiritual thermostat runs cold. Cold prayers always freeze before they reach heaven. Such cold devotions will have an adverse effect on anything you think you may be useful for. Doing good is to the whole household of faith. It is not about one person (your friend or buddy at church). It is not directed only to singular people. It has nothing to do with who you like or who you don't. It has to do with God who sends his people to minister to others. What do you have that others need? What do you have that

God sends you to them? Have you taken a tally of service to God? No Christian is exempt in this.

Sometimes doing good is hindered by inactivity. Athletes who train for a competition must train their muscles so that they are effective, so that they have a chance to be used. Christians must use their gifts so that they are exercised. Exercising their gifts builds those spiritual muscles up so that they can use them more, so that they can use them *period.* Atrophy occurs when muscles lay dormant. They lose their strength and their vigor. You are no different if you do not exercise what spiritual gifts you have to the household of faith. There is plenty of opportunity for you if you are looking in the right place.

I give you four practical reasons for growing weary, in brief. First, you may not be spiritually ready. If a believer would establish himself in spiritual readiness, he must grow in grace daily. He must continually endeavor, in God's grace, to grow stronger and stronger, and abound more and more in the exercise of his personal communion with God. They should, at all times, to grow inwardly, by faith and love, hold on to Christ more firmly for all their gracious influences; to grow outwardly, by being more and more fruitful in good works; to grow up in heavenly mindedness and eternal joy in God. At the same time, in order to do good with all spiritual readiness, you should also be continually on guard against sinning, and the manner in which you use and enjoy lawful things. Too much of the world will hinder your usefulness to Christ.

Second, not doing good as God orders it. *Your way of doing* is not better than Scriptures. Whatever it is that you do, do it with all your might, but do it as God so orders it. Do not be like Saul who thought it was up to him to order the way he would worship God after his return from the task of dealing with the Amalekites. Remember that his kingdom was ripped from him for not doing *what God so ordered*, "And Samuel said to Saul, Thou hast done foolishly: thou hast not kept the commandment of the LORD thy God, which he commanded thee," (1 Sam. 13:13). As the expression goes, *it is God's way or the highway.* This can even be seen in the friends of Job. They came to comfort him, but not in the right way. They were *miserable* comforters. They got into trouble with God for not knowing how to comfort their friend. What ill service!

Third, expecting immediate results. Never think that your timetable is God's timetable when it comes to reaping a harvest. "But, beloved, do not forget this one thing, that with the Lord one day is as a thousand years, and a thousand years as one day," (2 Peter 3:8). God is always good about bringing fruit in just the right time. If one, then, is resting on God's providence, and not their desires, all things work out accordingly. But if you try and press your will over God's will, well, we find a great many problems occurring in Scripture when people become impatient, and wearied at waiting on God.

Consider Abraham, Ishmael, Sarah, Hagar and that tiresome situation where Sarah decided to *help God out* with a remedy for gaining a holy heir. Say with Paul, "I planted, Apollos watered, but God gave the increase," (1 Cor. 3:6), expecting not only immediate results, but results in a certain timetable. Oftentimes we read things in the bible that seem fast. Read one of the Gospels, and the life of Jesus seems to go by very fast. Read Exodus and you find things moving very fast. Read Acts, and you find all kinds of growth in the church happening very fast. Fast is *relative*, in things that often take years to see fruit. The parable of the seeds and soil (Matt. 13:18ff) on the various grounds is not something to determine inside a week. Give such growth five years, or eight. Give it some time. Plants take time to grow. In our generation we often want things done *fast*. We want buildings built fast, food prepared fast, work weeks to fly by fast, and conveniences of all kinds dished out fast. But we must wait for God's timetable and not grow weary in our doing good to others as it pertains to eternal realities, for if we work in God's time, we will reap a reward.

Lastly, dealing with difficult situations or people in ministry. For ministers, dealing with difficult people makes a quick work of a minister sometimes, or even over a period of years. It will whittle him down, especially if his livelihood is dependent on the people of the church to pay bills and feed his family. For those in church, whenever there are episodes of personalities at work, or politics that arises between church factions, there too you find people whittled down. It makes doing good very hard, and wearies the soul set out to give others a blessing.

Meditate on your *resolute service* and your *resolved stamina* in the work of doing good. Do not grow weary in well doing. Know that as you submit to the will of God, you will fall into accordance to his will in service, if you *faint not.*

FINIS

Other Books in the 5 Marks Series at Puritan Publications

5 Marks of Devotion to God
Do you long for a closer relationship to the Savior Jesus Christ? Do you desire a more intimate communion with God each day? Every true Christian does. Mark 1: Daily Bible Reading and Study, Mark 2: Daily Meditation, Mark 3: Daily Prayer, Mark 4: Fasting, Mark 5: Family Worship.

5 Marks of Biblical Reformation
Everybody loves to claim the magisterial reformation for their own! Everyone wants to be a reformer in that way. But take God's principles of a Biblical Reformation and apply them to the church in practical daily living, then that's a different story all together. Mark 1: Spiritual Growth in Biblical Reformation. Mark 2: Guarding the Heart and True Biblical Reform. Mark 3: Rejecting Partial Reformation as Sin and a Full Offense to God. Mark 4: Reformation and Prayer. Mark 5: The Spirit in Biblical Reformation.

5 Marks of Biblical Commitment to the Visible Body of Christ
Are you a member of Christ's church? Are you a covenanter? Do you support your church? Are you committed to it? How do you show it? Mark 1: Gospel Unity. Mark 2: Public Prayer. Mark 3: Tithing and Support. Mark 4: Gospel Worship. Part 2. Mark 5: Church Membership

5 Marks of a Biblical Disciple
What is a disciple? A disciple has "5 Marks" outlined in Scripture which demonstrate a Spirit-filled walking with Jesus Christ in newness of life. Mark 1: Gospel Love, which is the badge of the

Christian. Mark 2: Gospel Interest, which glorifies God through Christ in truth and the power of the Spirit to be used to expand the kingdom of God. Mark 3: Gospel Consolation, which exercises a consoling spirit between believers. Mark 4: Gospel Encouragement, which is to encourage one another in the faith while it is still called today. Mark 5: Gospel Fellowship, which brings together disciples under the commonness of covenanted blessings both with God, and with other believers in a local church.

5 Marks of a Biblical Church

What are the marks of a biblical church? There are 5 marks that demonstrate the church as the pillar and ground of the truth. Mark 1: Biblical Preaching Through Sound Doctrine. Mark 2: Biblical Administration of the Sacraments. Mark 3: Biblical Administration of Church Discipline. Mark 4: Biblical Leadership. Mark 5: Biblical Worship.

www.ingramcontent.com/pod-product-compliance
Lightning Source LLC
Chambersburg PA
CBHW070200100426
42743CB00013B/2992